GRIMMY
Inc.

My Dad
Was a Boxer

by Mi

TOR®

A TOM DOHERTY ASSOCIATES BOOK
NEW YORK

This is a work of fiction. All the characters and events portrayed in this book are either products of the author's imagination or are used fictitiously.

GRIMMY™: MY DAD WAS A BOXER

™ and copyright © 1999 by Grimmy, Inc. All rights reserved.

www.grimmy.com

This book contains material previously published in a trade edition as *Grimmy: King of the Heap*.

A Tor Book
Published by Tom Doherty Associates, LLC
175 Fifth Avenue
New York, NY 10010

www.tor.com

Tor® is a registered trademark of Tom Doherty Associates, LLC.

ISBN: 0-812-57461-3

First edition: November 1999

Printed in the United States of America

0 9 8 7 6 5 4 3 2 1

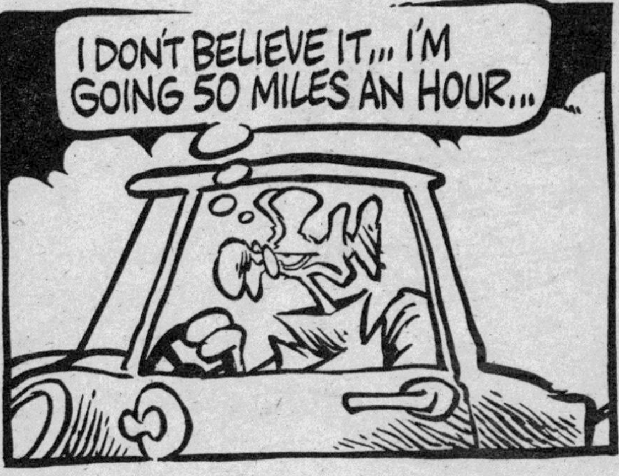
I DON'T BELIEVE IT,,, I'M GOING 50 MILES AN HOUR...

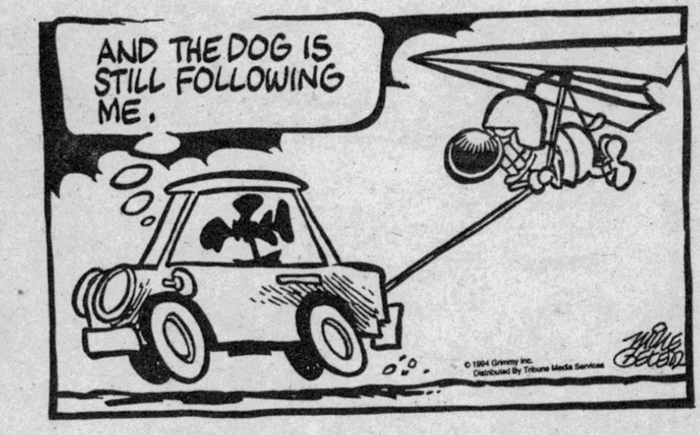
AND THE DOG IS STILL FOLLOWING ME.
© 1994 Grimmy Inc. Distributed By Tribune Media Services

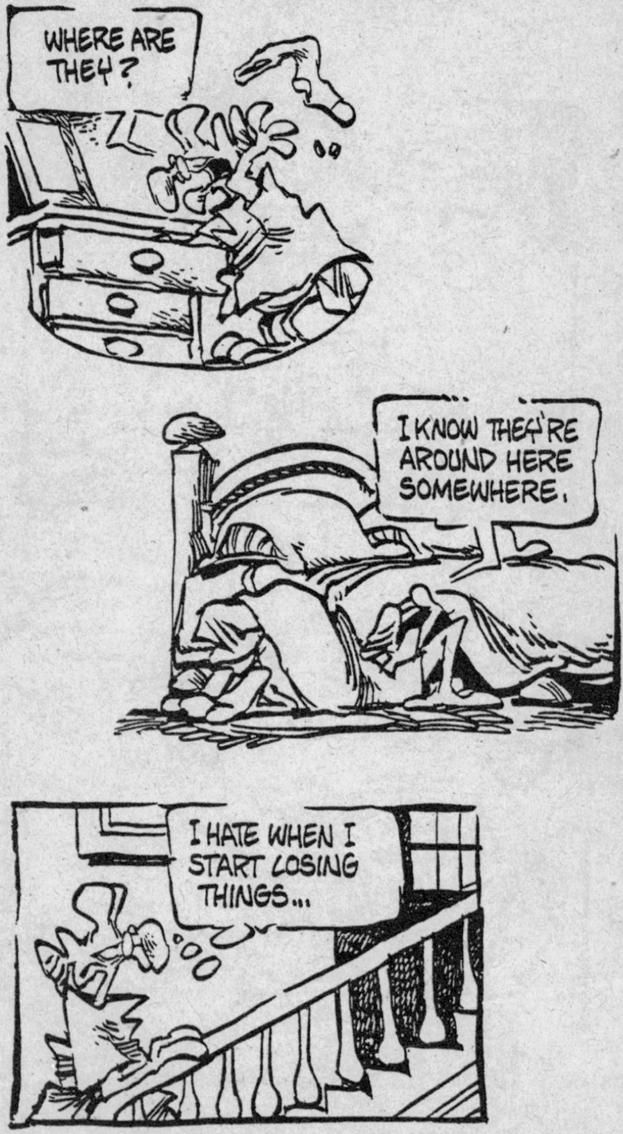
WHERE ARE THEY?
I KNOW THEY'RE AROUND HERE SOMEWHERE.
I HATE WHEN I START LOSING THINGS...

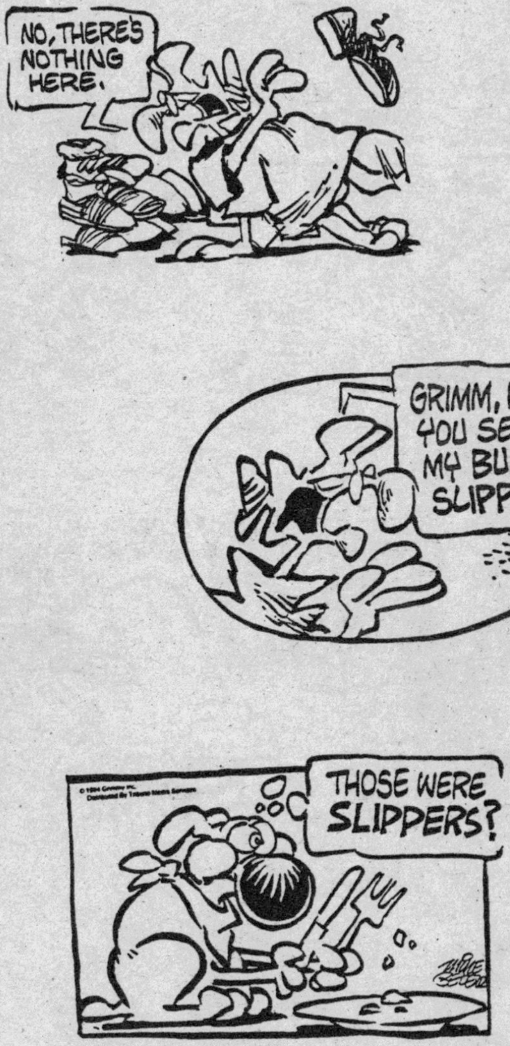
NO, THERE'S NOTHING HERE.
GRIMM, HAVE YOU SEEN MY BUNNY SLIPPERS?
THOSE WERE SLIPPERS?

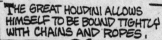

THE GREAT HOUDINI ALLOWS HIMSELF TO BE BOUND TIGHTLY WITH CHAINS AND ROPES.

KNOWN THROUGHOUT THE WORLD AS THE GREATEST LIVING ESCAPE ARTIST.

HE BEGINS SILENTLY TO FREE HIMSELF FROM HIS CONSTRAINS.

USING SUPER-HUMAN CONTROL, HE SLIPS THE ROPES DOWN OVER HIS ARMS TO HIS CHEST.

WORKING FEVERISHLY, HE SLITHERS LIKE A REPTILE UNTIL THE ROPES ARE DOWN AROUND HIS HIPS.

SUDDENLY, IN THE DARKNESS, SOMEONE CALLS HIS NAME...

GRIMMY, HOW DID YOU EVER GET YOUR COLLAR DOWN THERE?

HOUDINI NEVER TELLS.

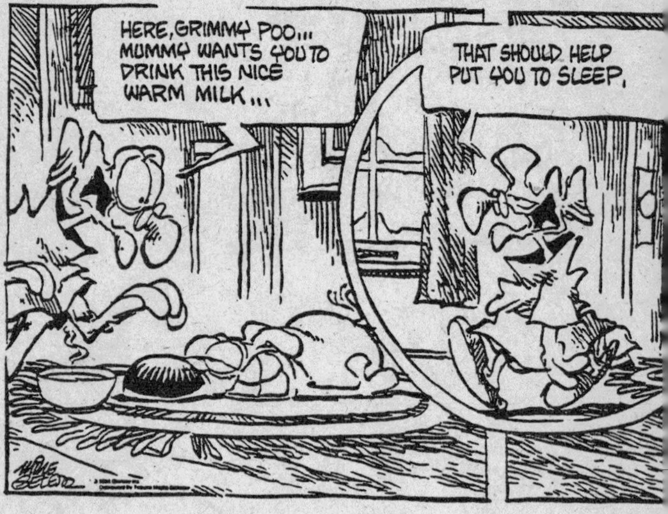
HERE, GRIMMY POO... MUMMY WANTS YOU TO DRINK THIS NICE WARM MILK...
THAT SHOULD HELP PUT YOU TO SLEEP.

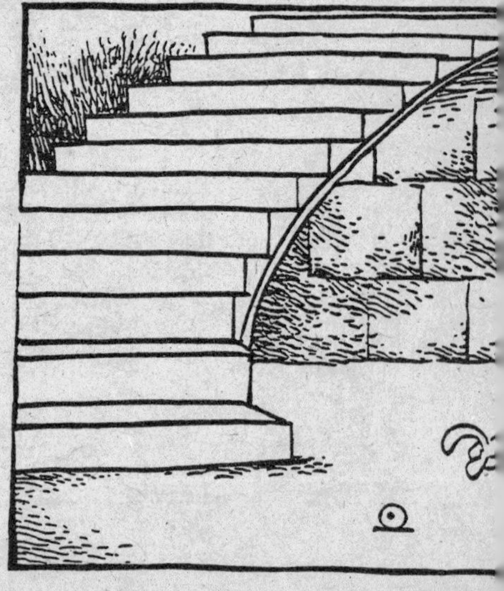

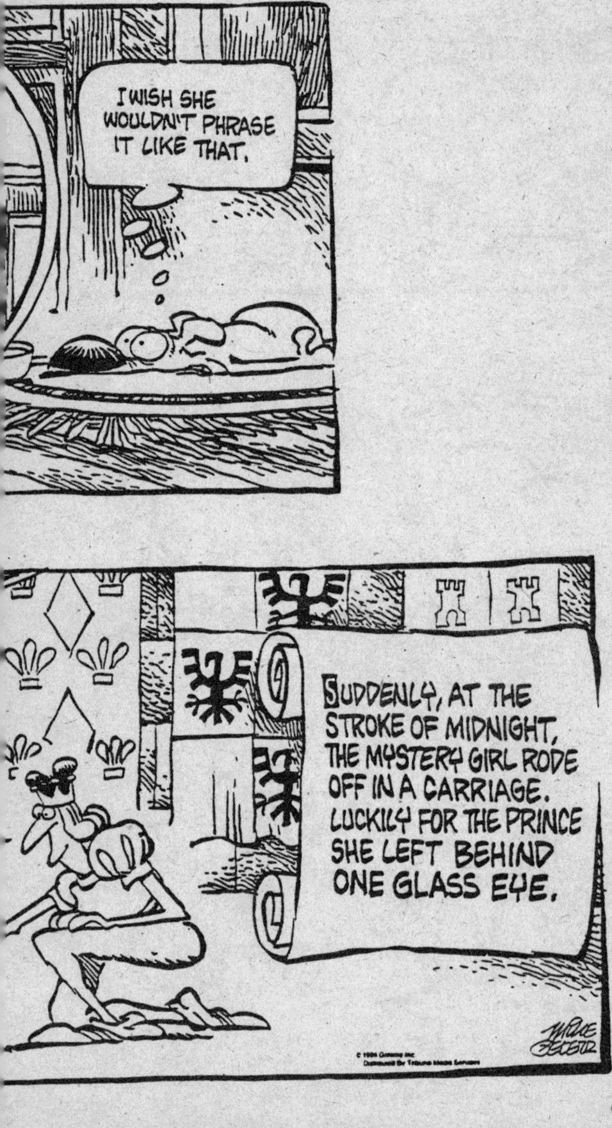
I WISH SHE WOULDN'T PHRASE IT LIKE THAT.
SUDDENLY, AT THE STROKE OF MIDNIGHT, THE MYSTERY GIRL RODE OFF IN A CARRIAGE. LUCKILY FOR THE PRINCE SHE LEFT BEHIND ONE GLASS EYE.

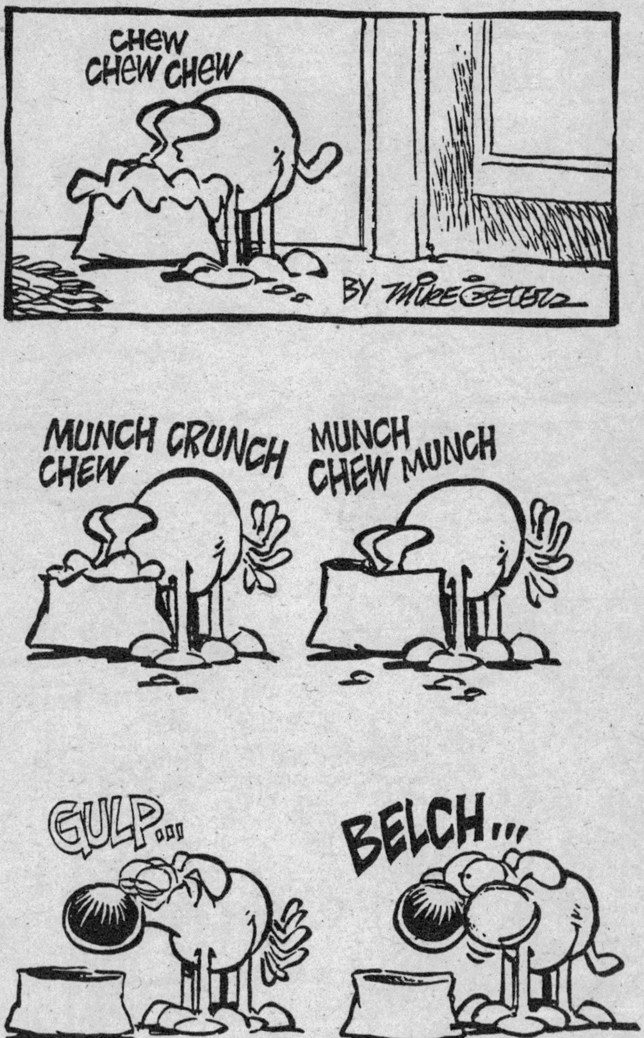

CHEW
CHEW CHEW
BY MIKE PETERS
MUNCH CRUNCH
CHEW
MUNCH
CHEW MUNCH
GULP...
BELCH...

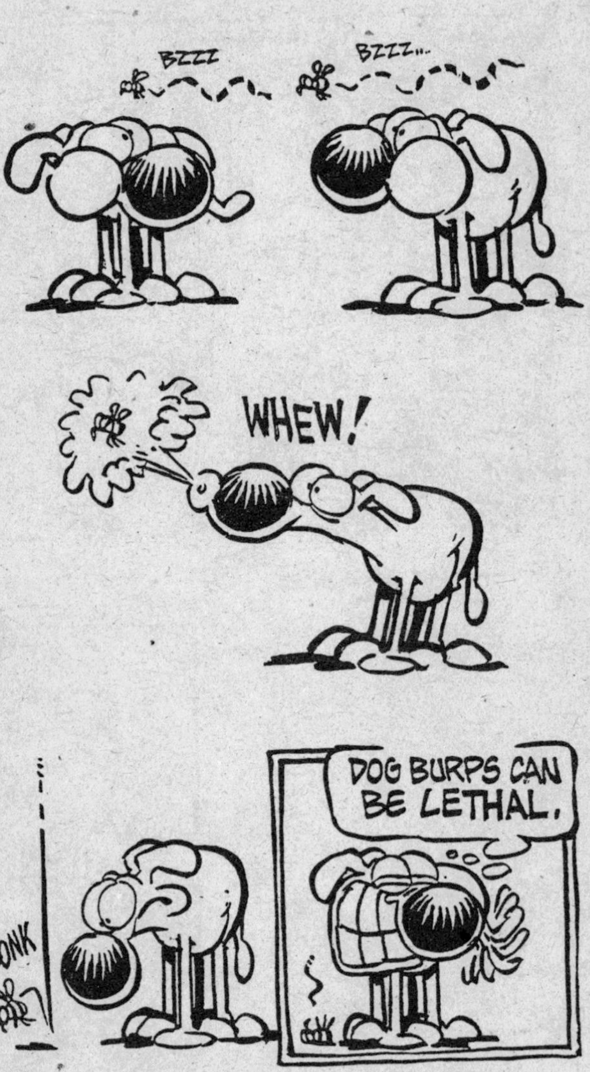
BZZZ
BZZZ...
WHEW!
BONK
DOG BURPS CAN BE LETHAL.

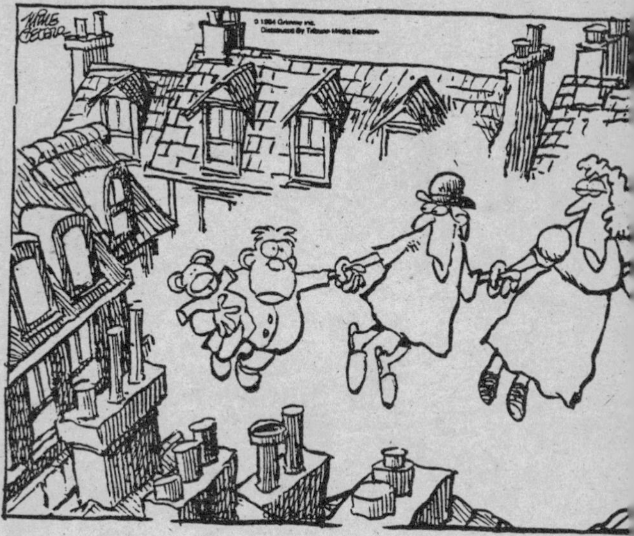

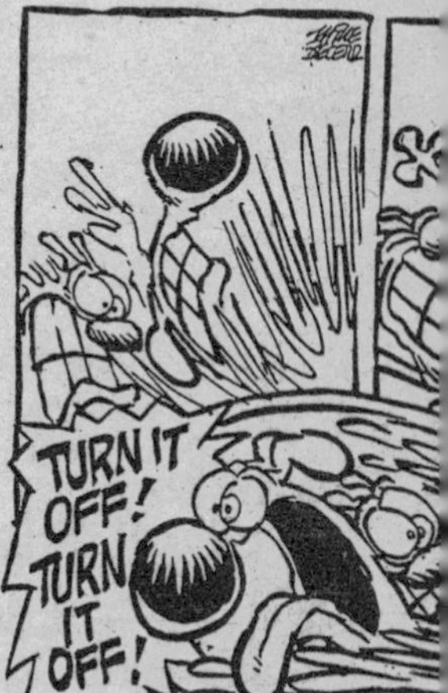
TURN IT OFF! TURN IT OFF!

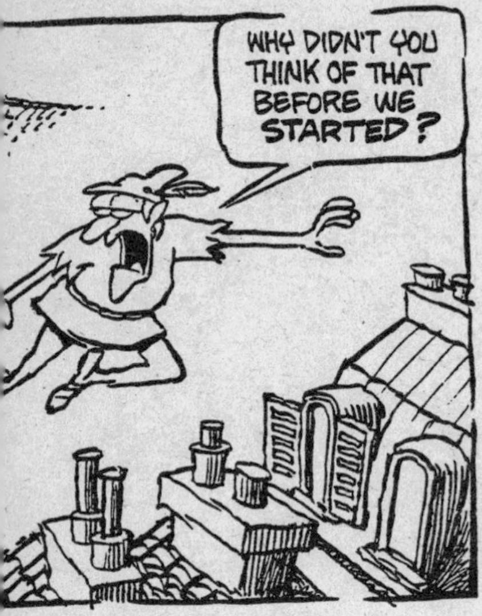
WHY DIDN'T YOU THINK OF THAT BEFORE WE STARTED?

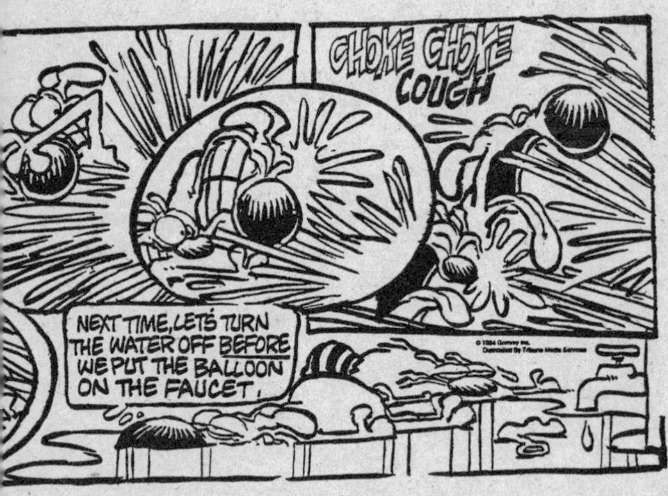
CHOKE CHOKE
COUGH
NEXT TIME, LET'S TURN THE WATER OFF BEFORE WE PUT THE BALLOON ON THE FAUCET.

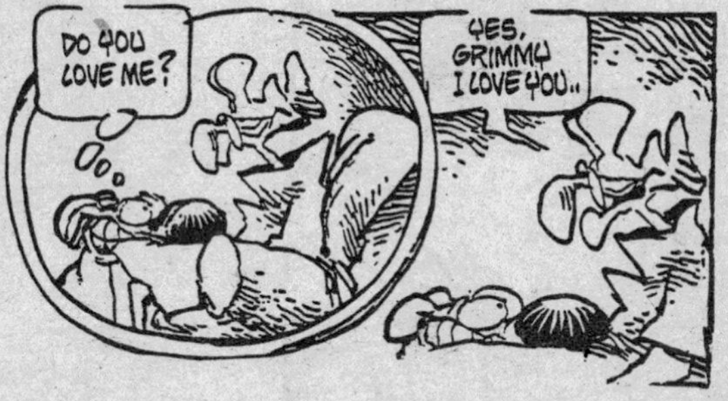
DO YOU LOVE ME?
YES, GRIMMY I LOVE YOU..

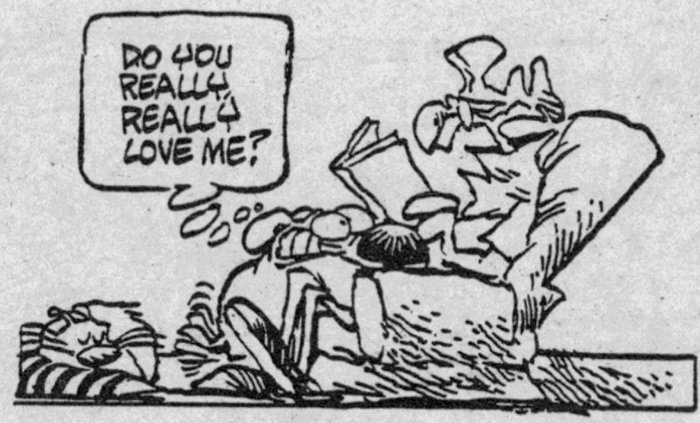
DO YOU REALLY, REALLY LOVE ME?

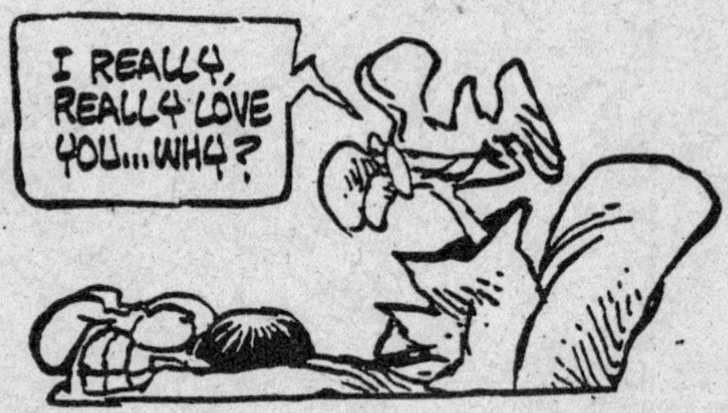
I REALLY, REALLY LOVE YOU... WHY?

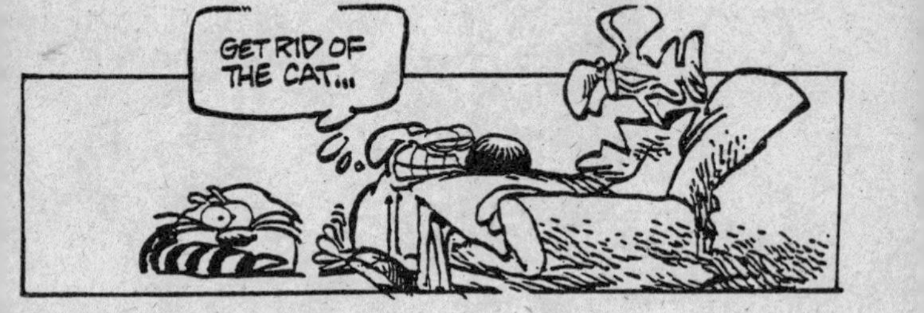
GET RID OF THE CAT...

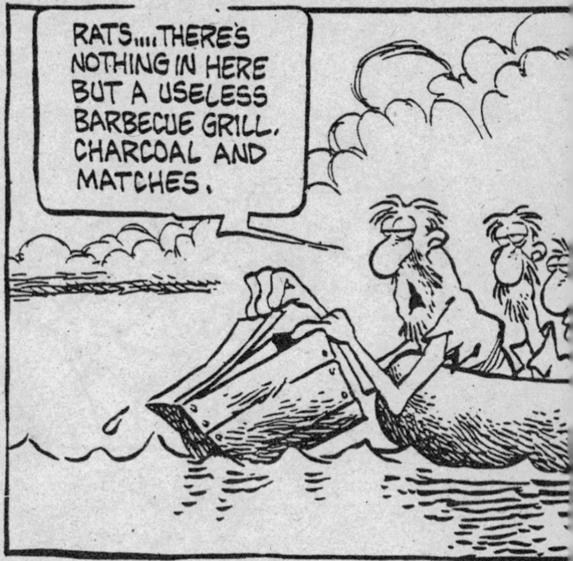
RATS....THERE'S NOTHING IN HERE BUT A USELESS BARBECUE GRILL, CHARCOAL AND MATCHES.

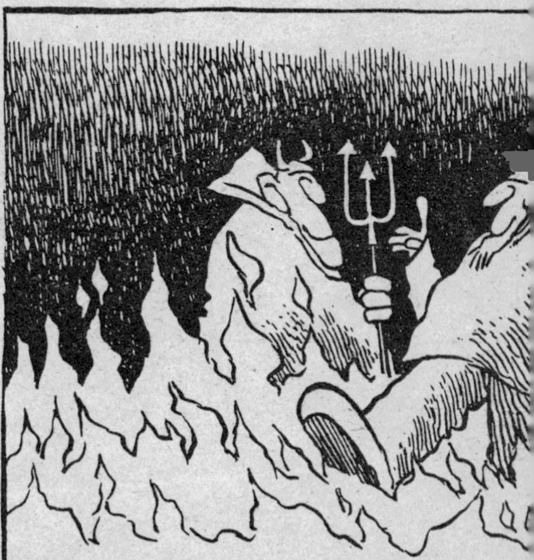

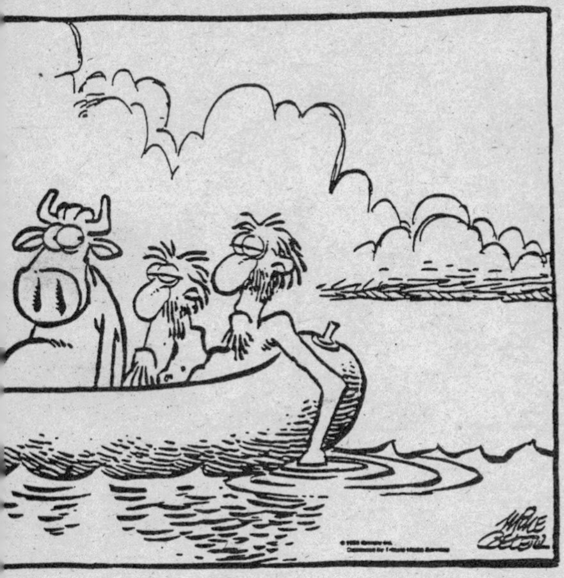

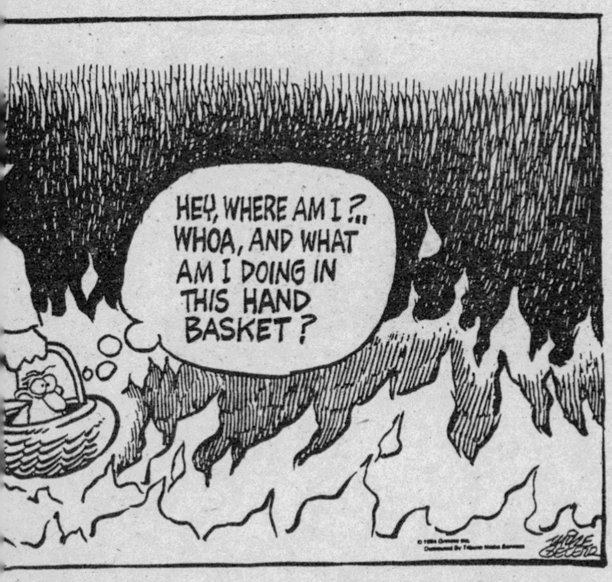
HEY, WHERE AM I ?... WHOA, AND WHAT AM I DOING IN THIS HAND BASKET ?

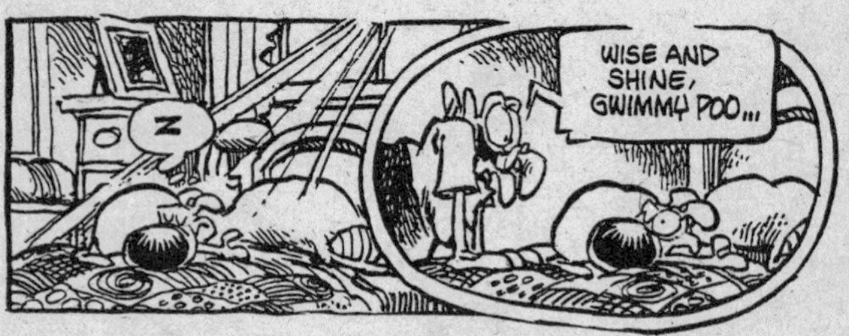
Z
WISE AND SHINE, GWIMMY POO...

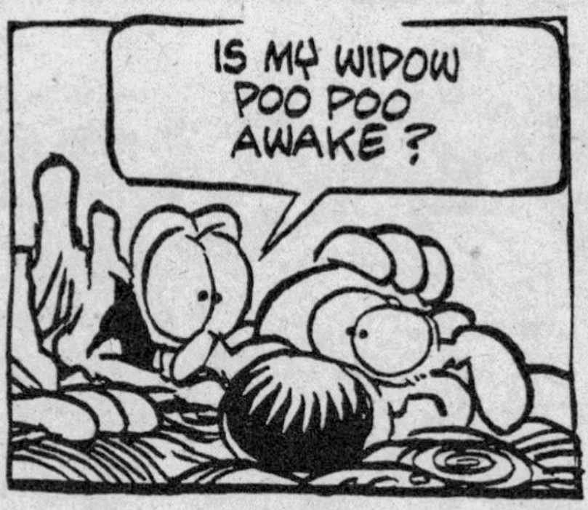
IS MY WIDOW POO POO AWAKE ?

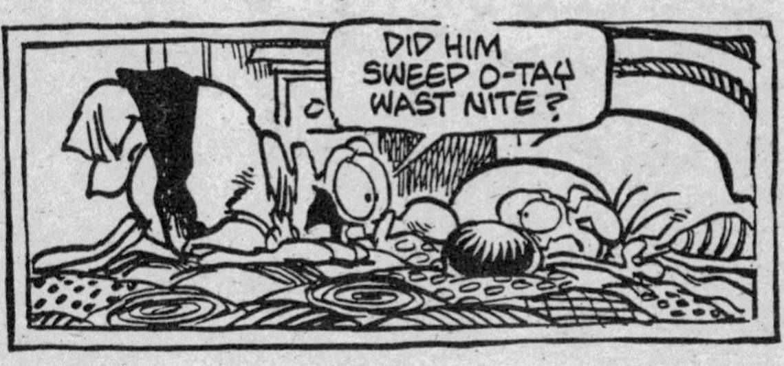
DID HIM SWEEP O-TAY WAST NITE?

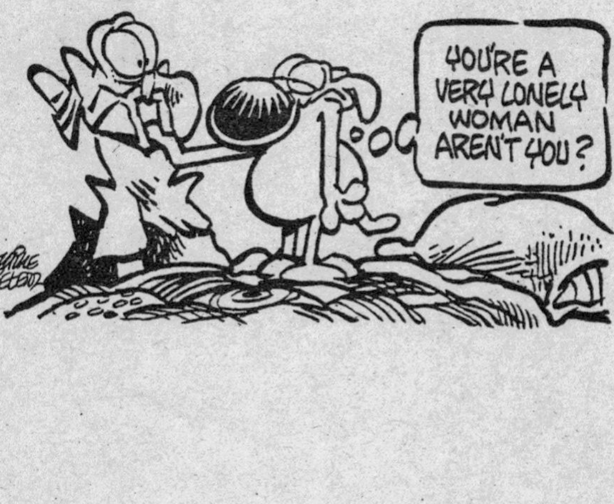
YOU'RE A VERY LONELY WOMAN AREN'T YOU?

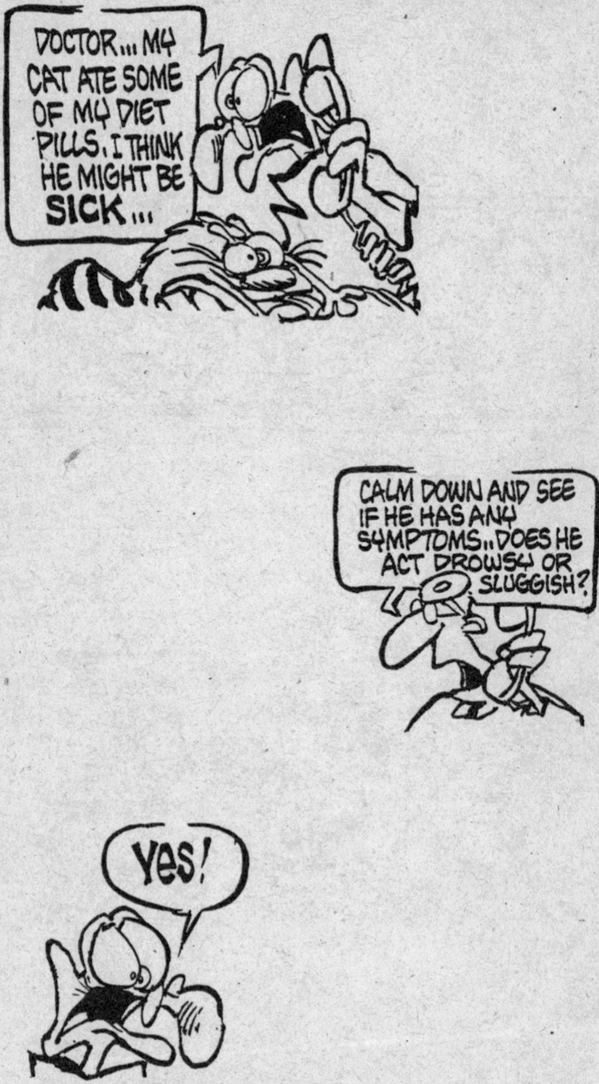
DOCTOR... MY CAT ATE SOME OF MY DIET PILLS. I THINK HE MIGHT BE **SICK**...
CALM DOWN AND SEE IF HE HAS ANY SYMPTOMS.. DOES HE ACT DROWSY OR SLUGGISH?
YES!

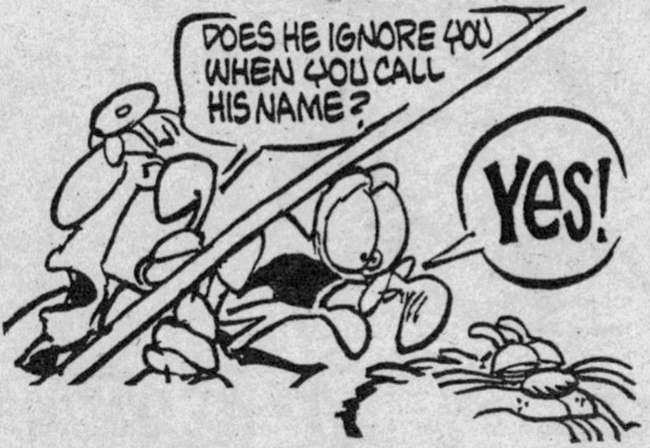
DOES HE IGNORE YOU WHEN YOU CALL HIS NAME?
YES!

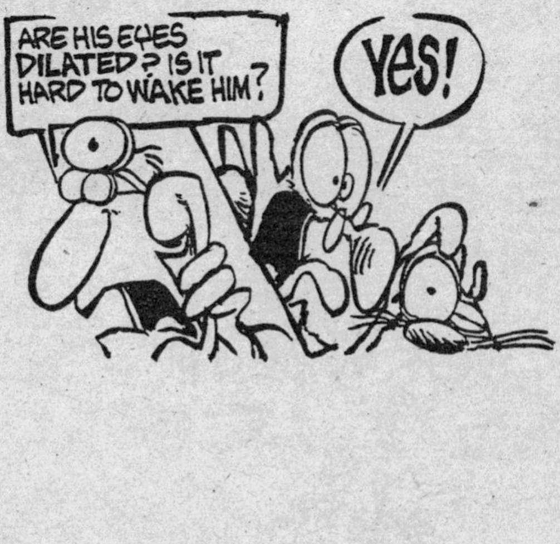
ARE HIS EYES DILATED? IS IT HARD TO WAKE HIM?
YES!

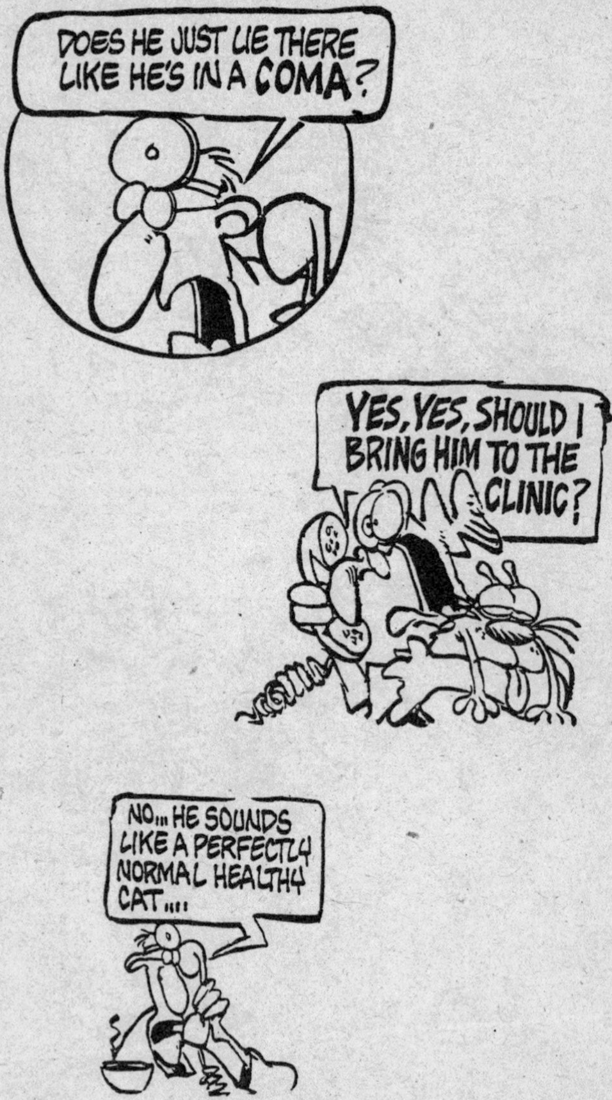
DOES HE JUST LIE THERE LIKE HE'S IN A COMA?
YES, YES, SHOULD I BRING HIM TO THE CLINIC?
NO... HE SOUNDS LIKE A PERFECTLY NORMAL HEALTHY CAT....

OKAY, GRIMMY, GO OUTSIDE AND PLAY.
HAVE FUN, BE GOOD...
WELL?... MAKE UP YOUR MIND.

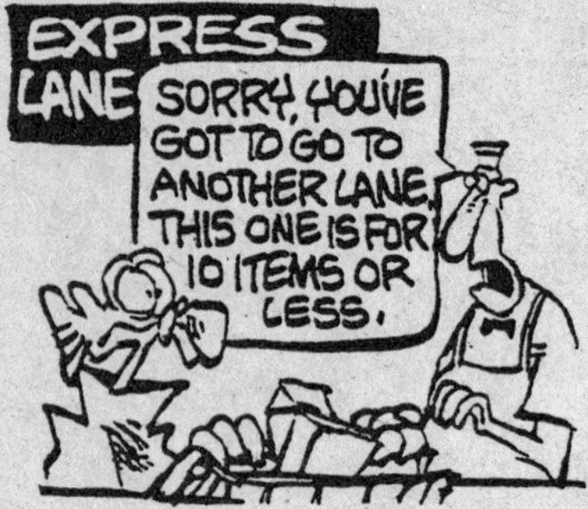
EXPRESS LANE
SORRY, YOU'VE GOT TO GO TO ANOTHER LANE. THIS ONE IS FOR 10 ITEMS OR LESS.

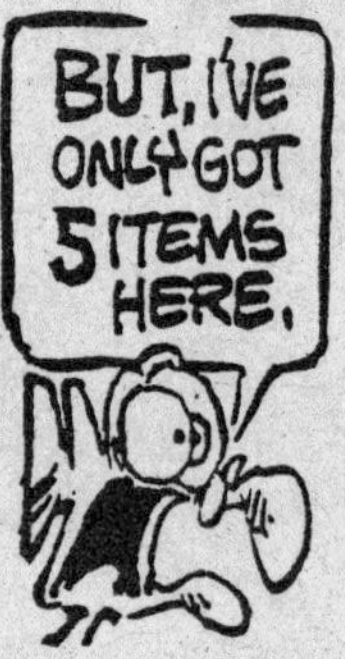
BUT, I'VE ONLY GOT 5 ITEMS HERE.

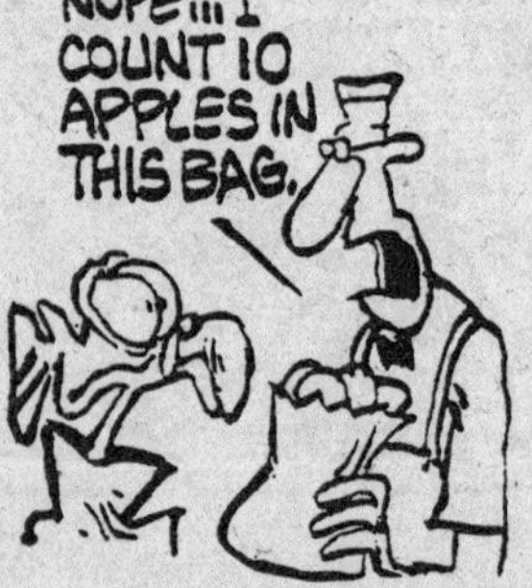
NOPE... I COUNT 10 APPLES IN THIS BAG.

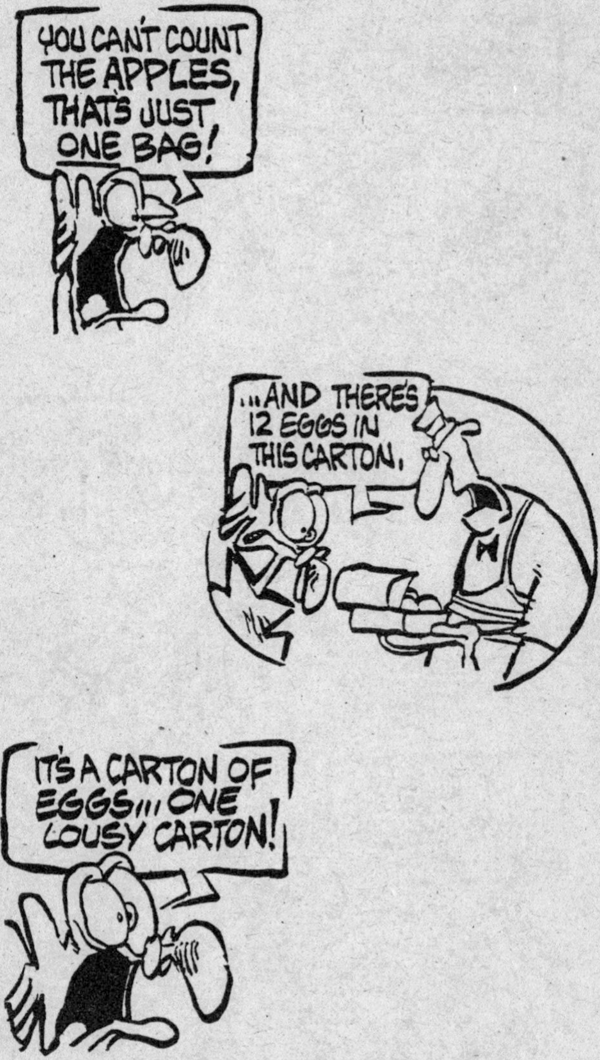
YOU CAN'T COUNT THE APPLES, THAT'S JUST ONE BAG!
...AND THERE'S 12 EGGS IN THIS CARTON.
IT'S A CARTON OF EGGS... ONE LOUSY CARTON!

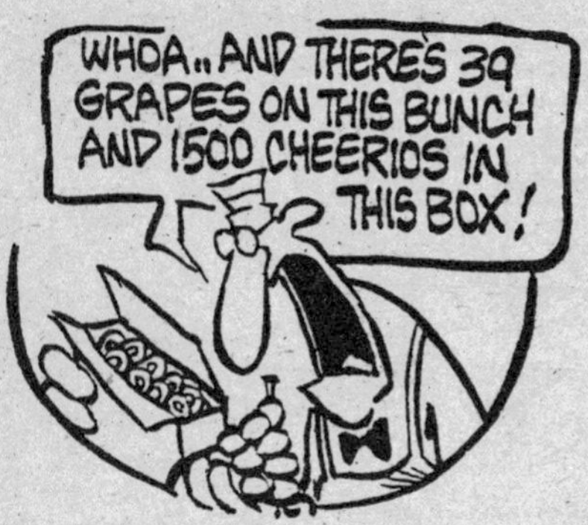
WHOA.. AND THERE'S 39 GRAPES ON THIS BUNCH AND 1500 CHEERIOS IN THIS BOX!

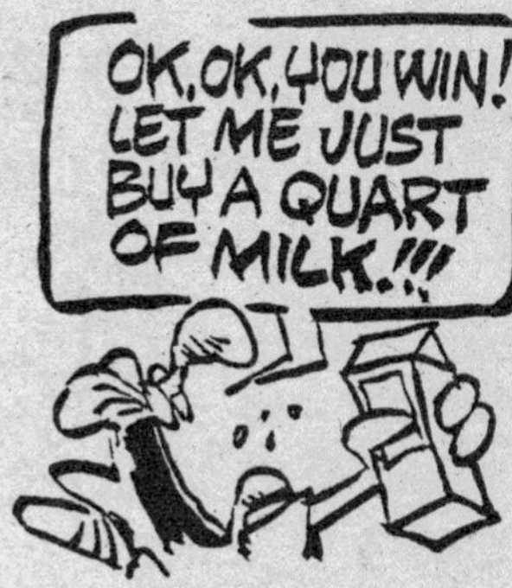
OK, OK, YOU WIN! LET ME JUST BUY A QUART OF MILK.!!!

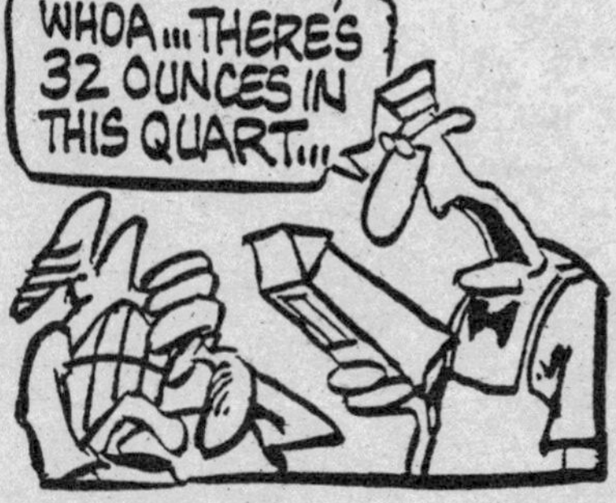
WHOA... THERE'S 32 OUNCES IN THIS QUART...

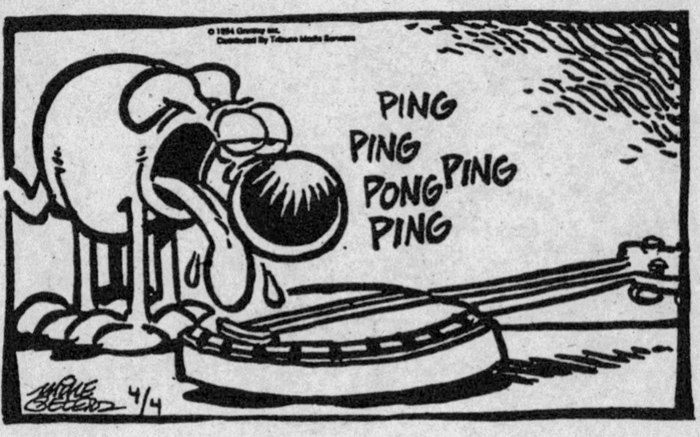
PING
PING
PONG
PING
PING

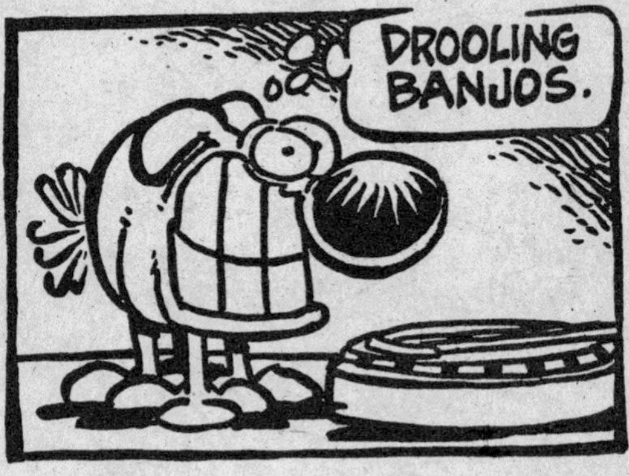
DROOLING BANJOS.

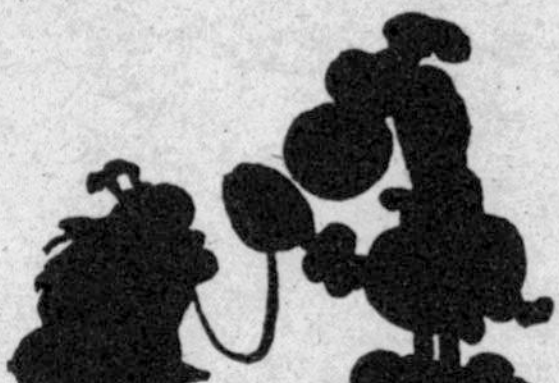

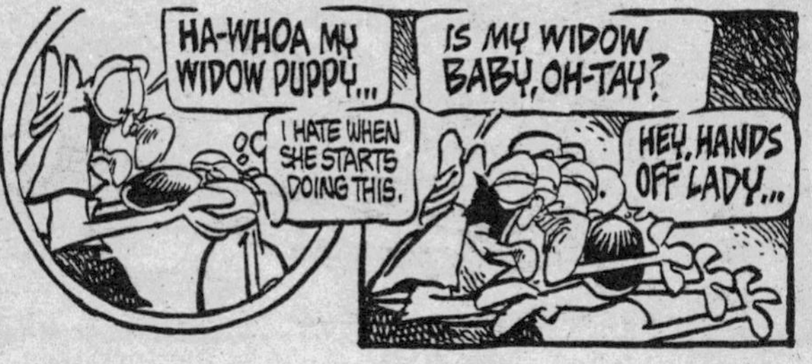
HA-WHOA MY WIDOW PUPPY...
I HATE WHEN SHE STARTS DOING THIS.
IS MY WIDOW BABY, OH-TAY?
HEY, HANDS OFF LADY...

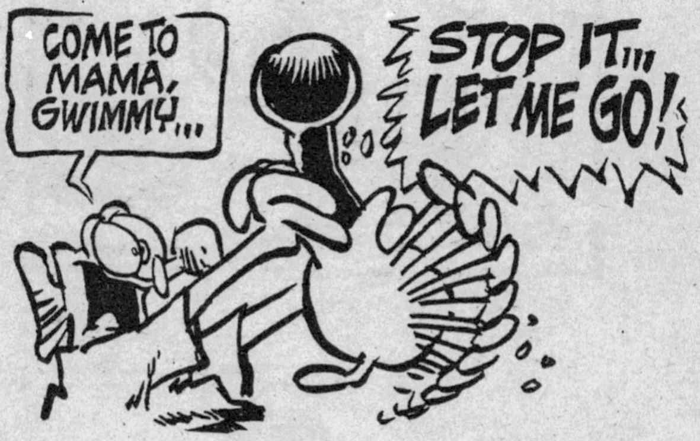
COME TO MAMA, GWIMMY...
STOP IT... LET ME GO!

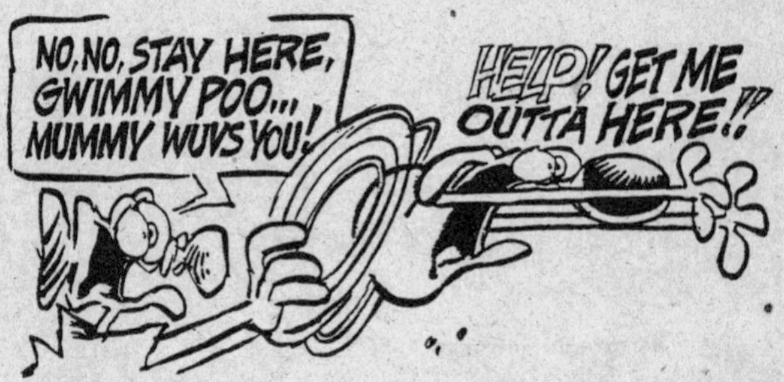
NO, NO, STAY HERE, GWIMMY POO..., MUMMY WUVS YOU!
HELP! GET ME OUTTA HERE!!

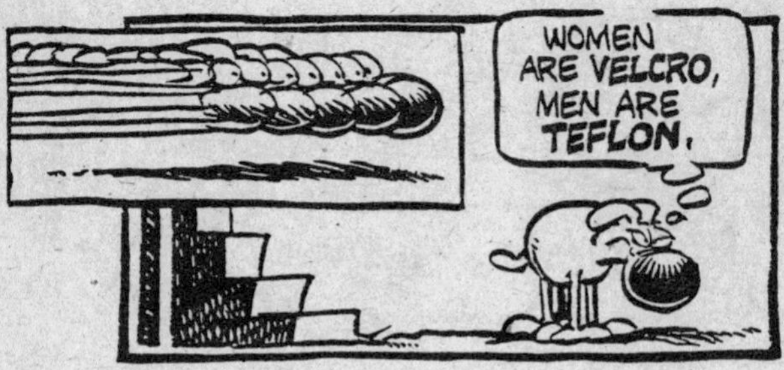
WOMEN ARE VELCRO, MEN ARE TEFLON.

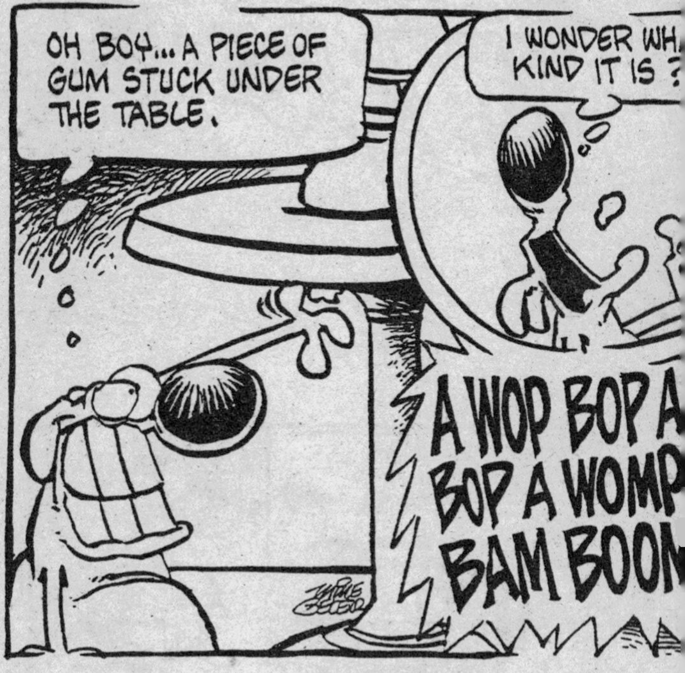
OH BOY... A PIECE OF GUM STUCK UNDER THE TABLE.
I WONDER WH
KIND IT IS ?
A WOP BOP A
BOP A WOMP
BAM BOOM

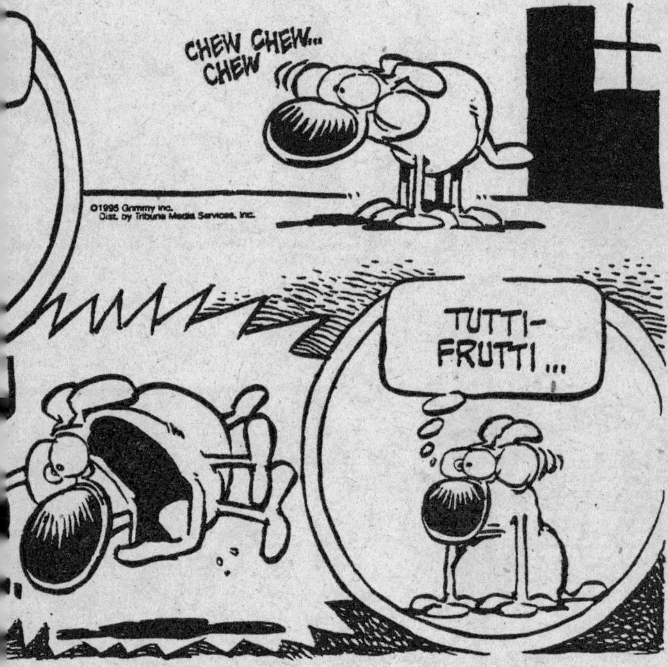
CHEW CHEW...
CHEW
TUTTI-
FRUTTI ...

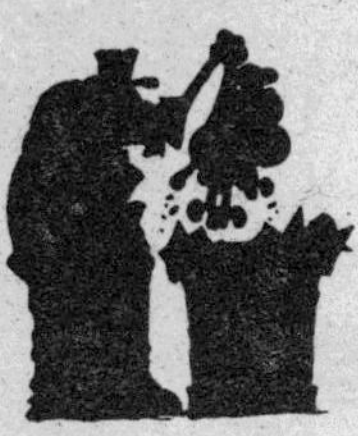

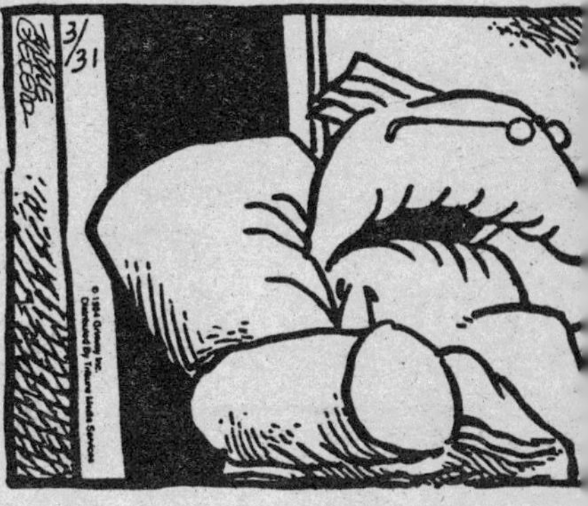
3/31
© 1984 Grimmy Inc.
Distributed By Tribune Media Services

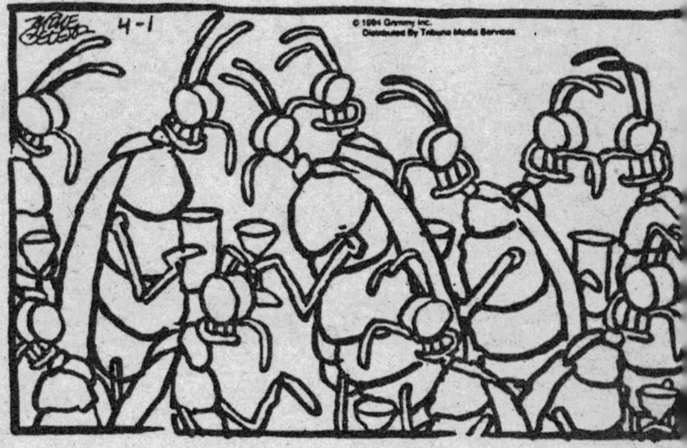
4-1
© 1984 Grimmy Inc.
Distributed By Tribune Media Services

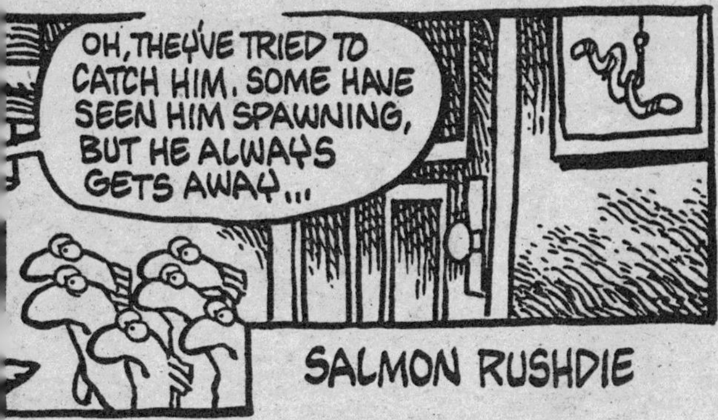
OH, THEY'VE TRIED TO CATCH HIM. SOME HAVE SEEN HIM SPAWNING, BUT HE ALWAYS GETS AWAY...
SALMON RUSHDIE

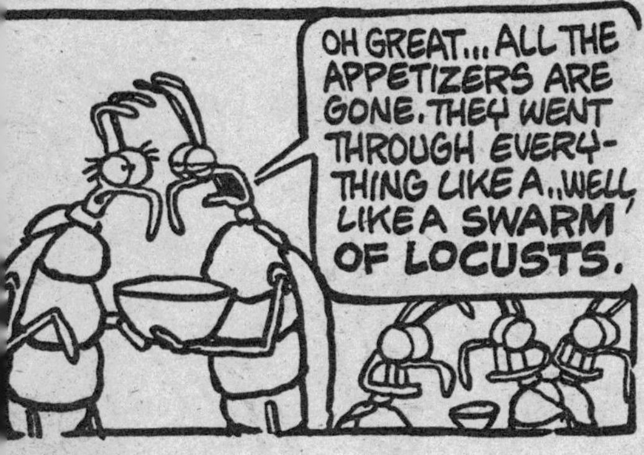
OH GREAT... ALL THE APPETIZERS ARE GONE. THEY WENT THROUGH EVERY-THING LIKE A.. WELL, LIKE A SWARM OF LOCUSTS.

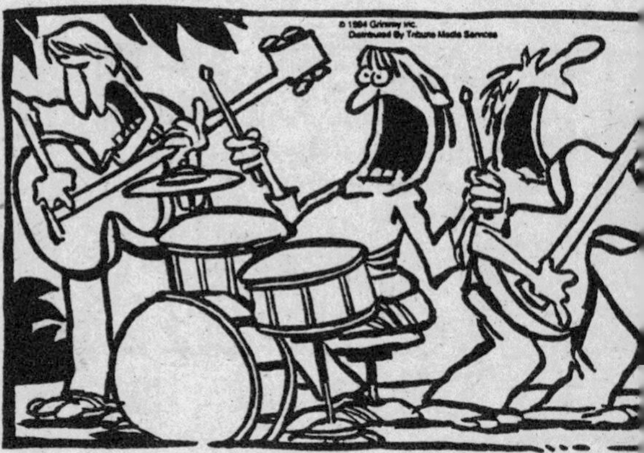
© 1994 Grimmy Inc.
Distributed By Tribune Media Services

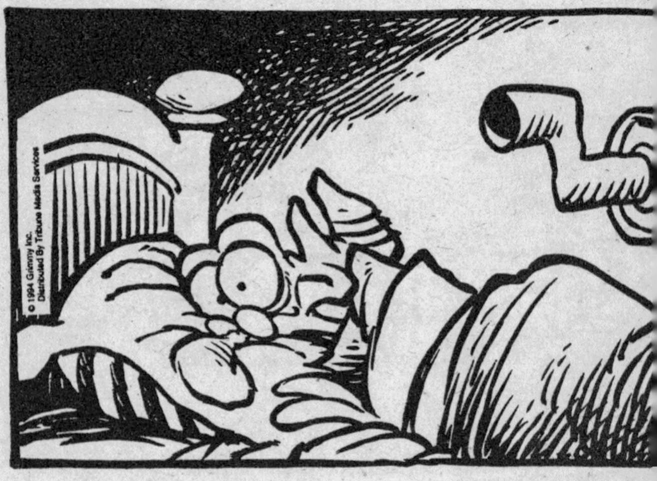
© 1994 Grimmy Inc.
Distributed By Tribune Media Services

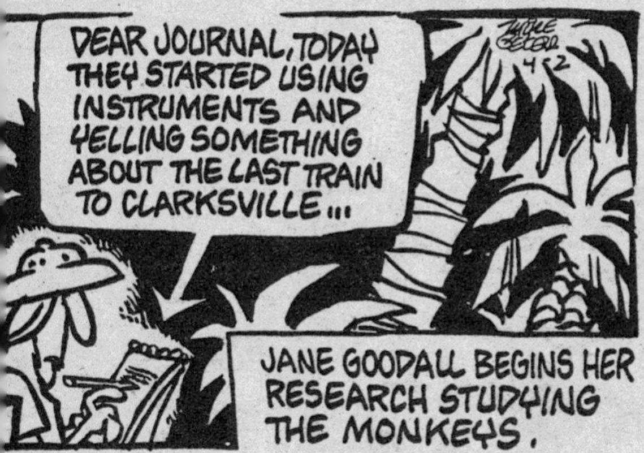
DEAR JOURNAL, TODAY THEY STARTED USING INSTRUMENTS AND YELLING SOMETHING ABOUT THE LAST TRAIN TO CLARKSVILLE...
JANE GOODALL BEGINS HER RESEARCH STUDYING THE MONKEYS.

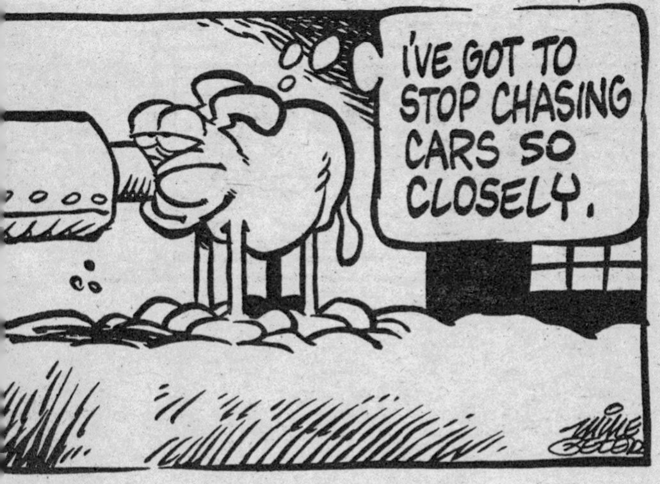
I'VE GOT TO STOP CHASING CARS SO CLOSELY.

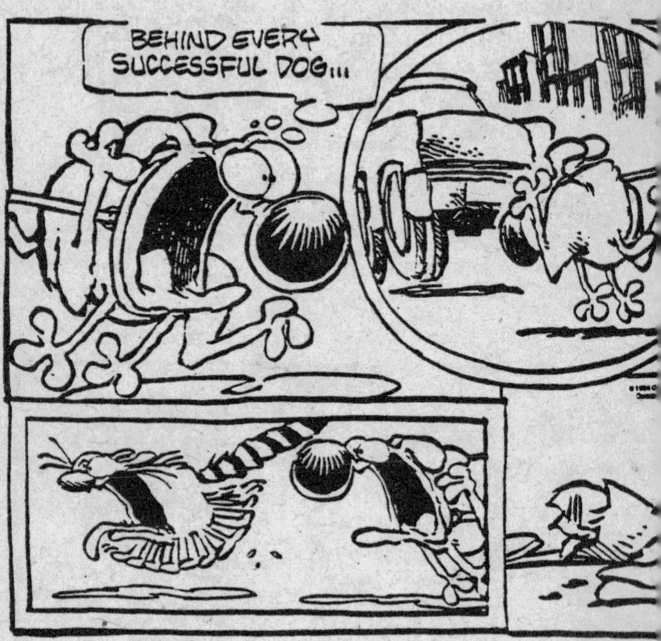
BEHIND EVERY SUCCESSFUL DOG...

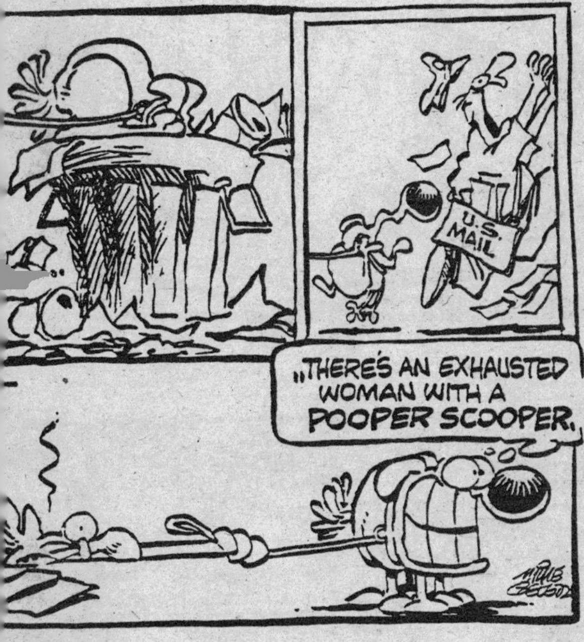
U.S. MAIL
..THERE'S AN EXHAUSTED WOMAN WITH A POOPER SCOOPER.

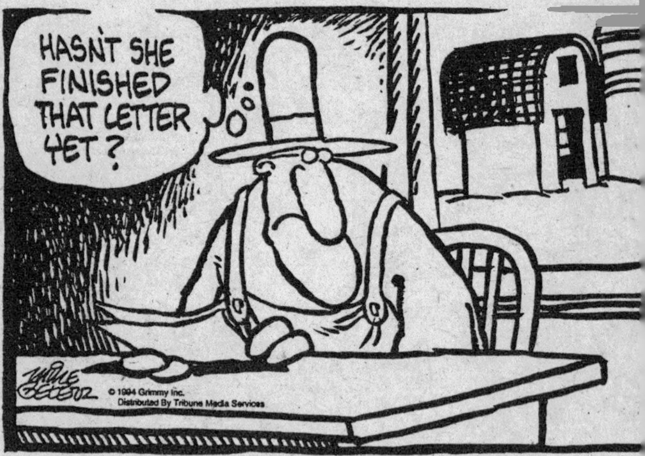
HASN'T SHE FINISHED THAT LETTER YET?
© 1994 Grimmy Inc.
Distributed By Tribune Media Services

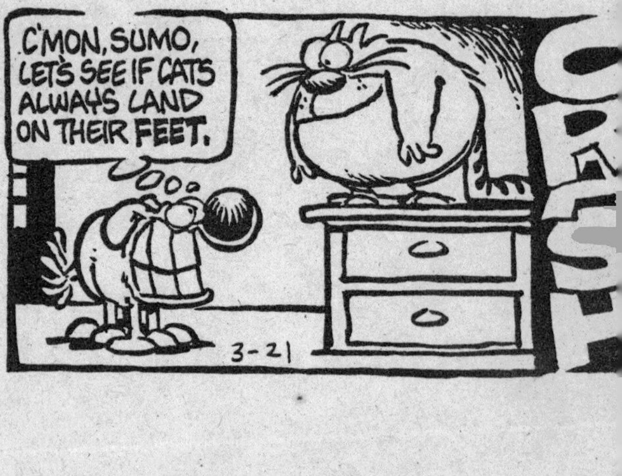
C'MON, SUMO, LET'S SEE IF CATS ALWAYS LAND ON THEIR FEET.
3-21

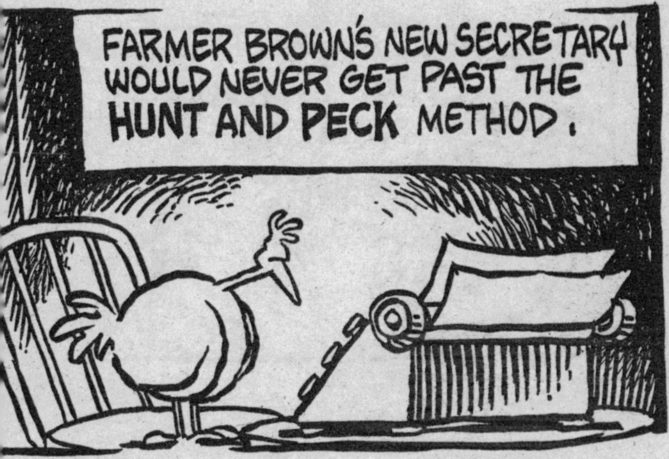
FARMER BROWN'S NEW SECRETARY WOULD NEVER GET PAST THE HUNT AND PECK METHOD.

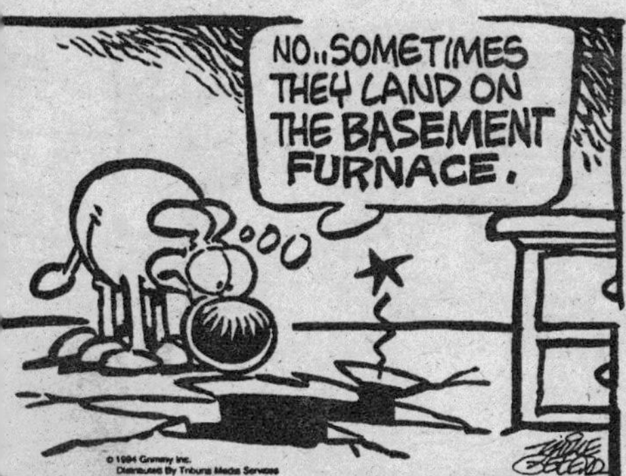
NO..SOMETIMES THEY LAND ON THE BASEMENT FURNACE.
OOO
© 1994 Grimmy Inc.
Distributed By Tribune Media Services

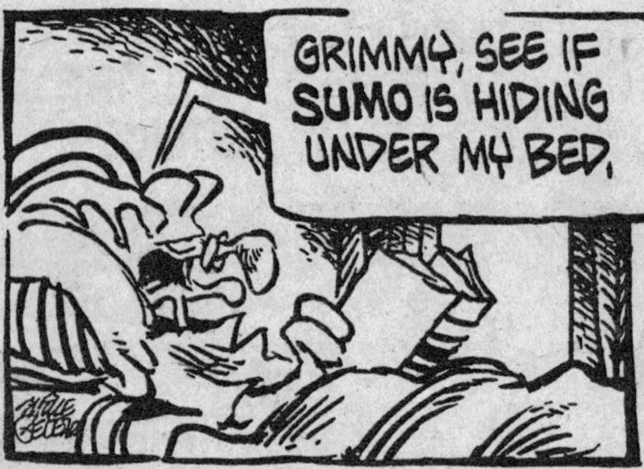
GRIMMY, SEE IF SUMO IS HIDING UNDER MY BED.

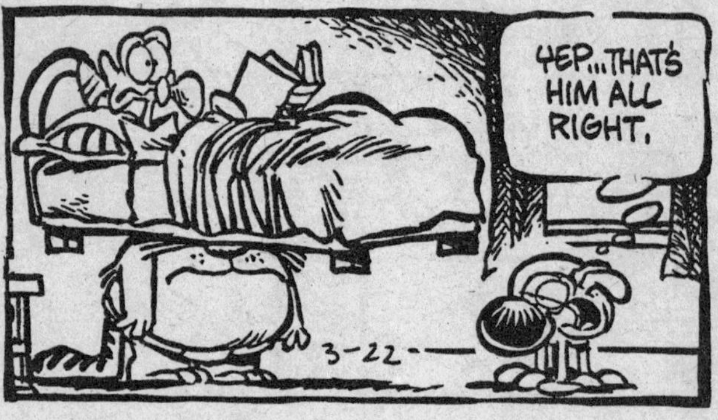
YEP...THAT'S HIM ALL RIGHT.
3-22

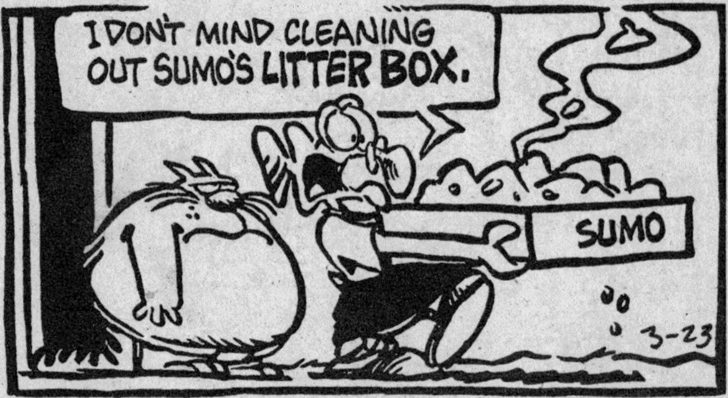
I DON'T MIND CLEANING OUT SUMO'S LITTER BOX.
SUMO
3-23

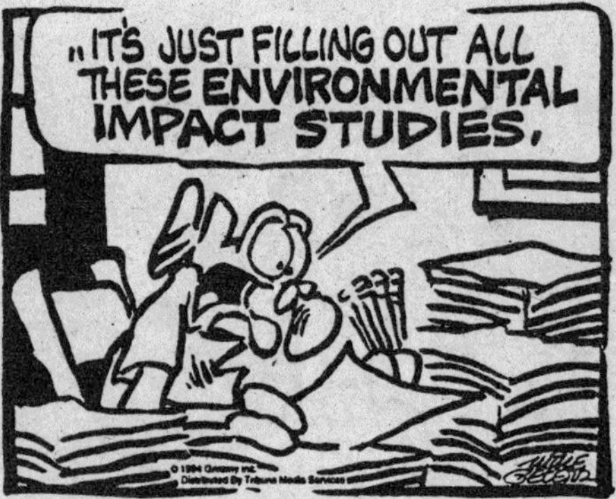
..IT'S JUST FILLING OUT ALL THESE ENVIRONMENTAL IMPACT STUDIES.
© 1994 Grimmy Inc.
Distributed By Tribune Media Services

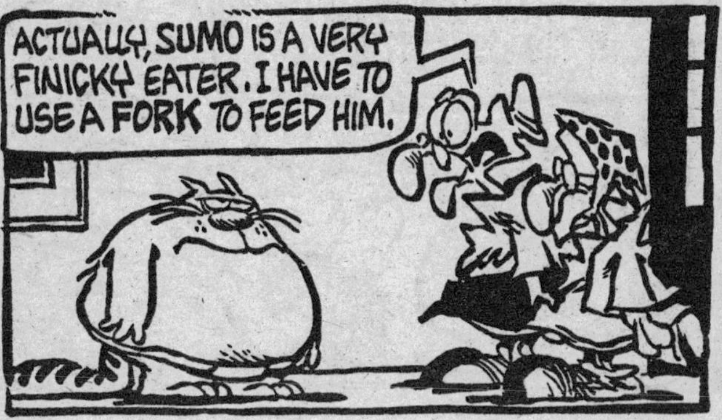
ACTUALLY, SUMO IS A VERY FINICKY EATER. I HAVE TO USE A FORK TO FEED HIM.

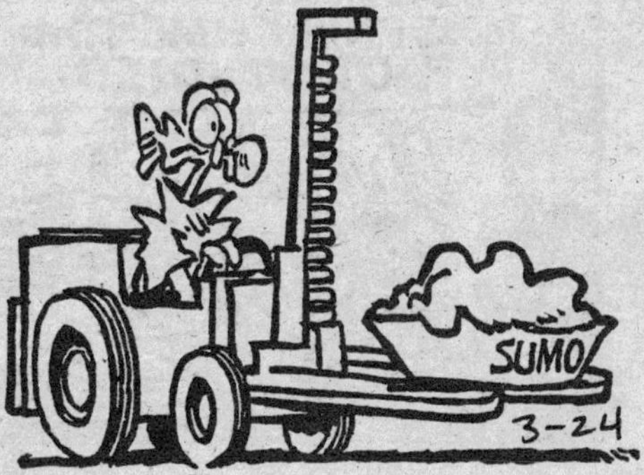
SUMO
3-24

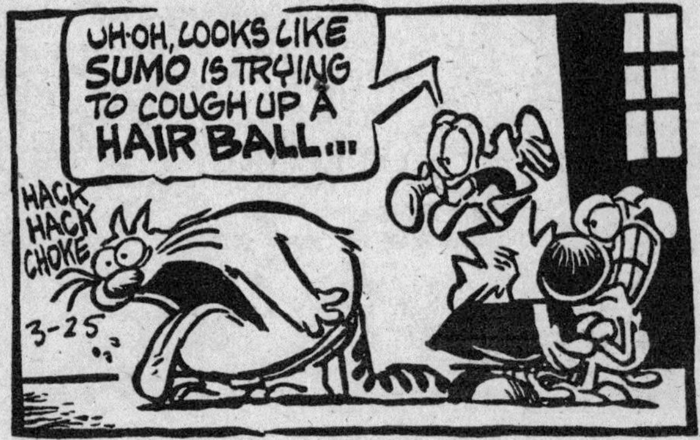
UH-OH, LOOKS LIKE SUMO IS TRYING TO COUGH UP A HAIR BALL...
HACK HACK CHOKE
3-25

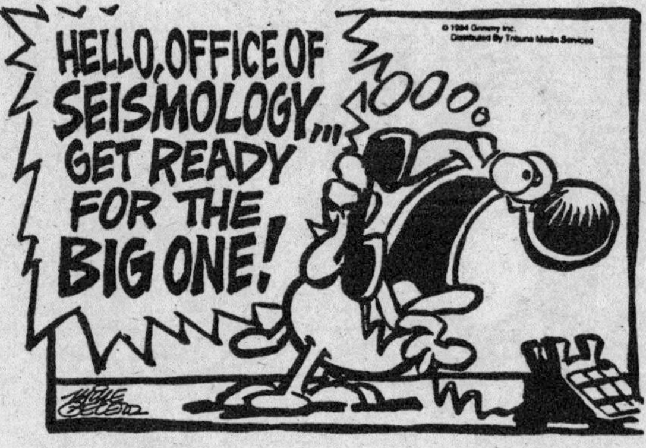
HELLO, OFFICE OF SEISMOLOGY... GET READY FOR THE BIG ONE!
OOOO
© 1994 Grimmy Inc.
Distributed By Tribune Media Services

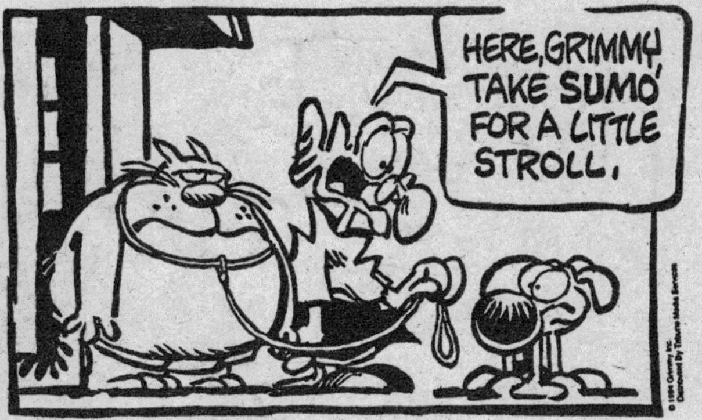
HERE, GRIMMY, TAKE SUMO FOR A LITTLE STROLL.

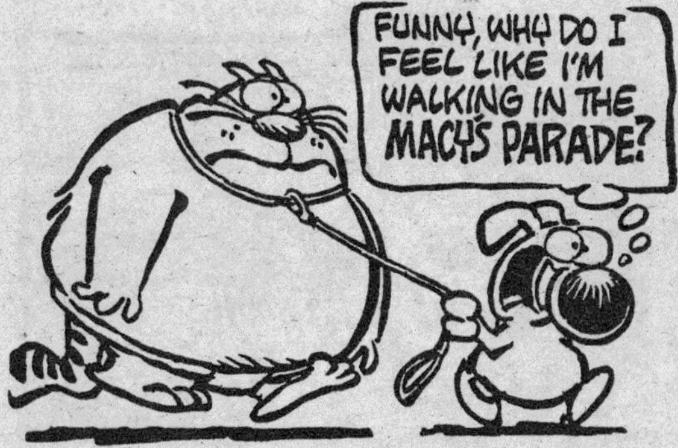
FUNNY, WHY DO I FEEL LIKE I'M WALKING IN THE MACY'S PARADE?

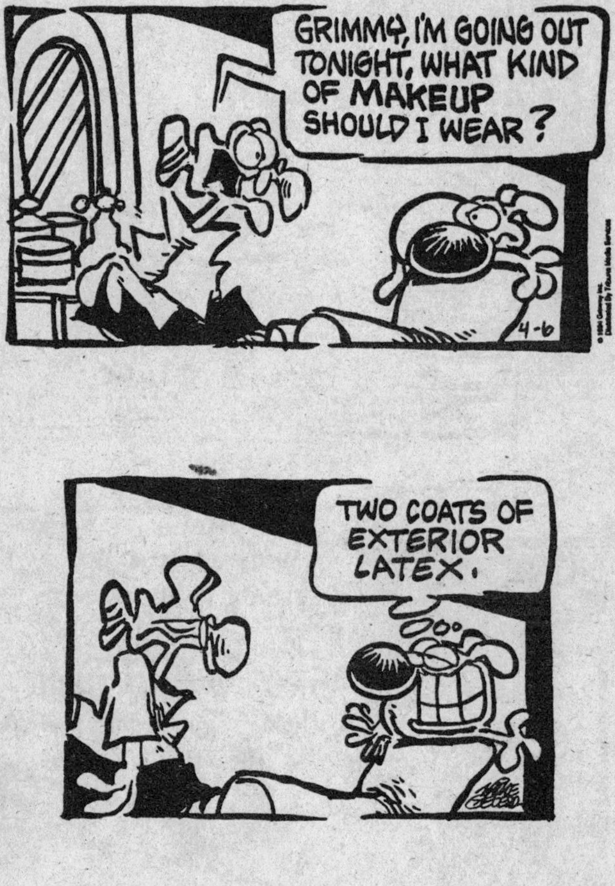
GRIMMY, I'M GOING OUT TONIGHT, WHAT KIND OF MAKEUP SHOULD I WEAR?
4-6
TWO COATS OF EXTERIOR LATEX.

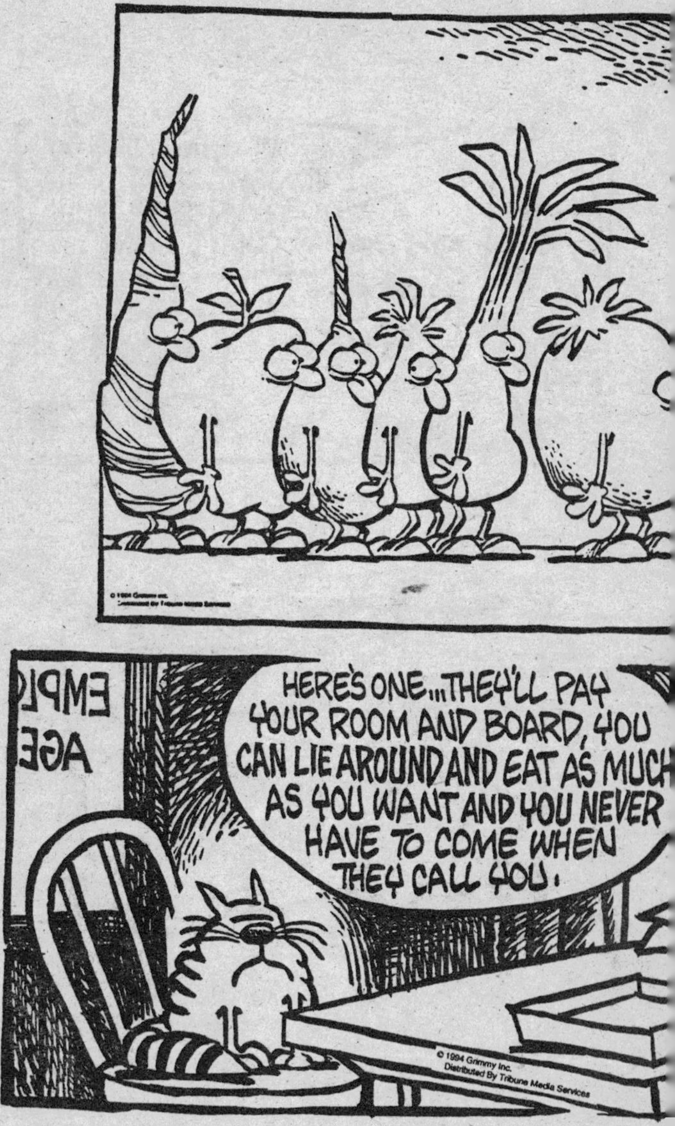
HERE'S ONE...THEY'LL PAY YOUR ROOM AND BOARD, YOU CAN LIE AROUND AND EAT AS MUCH AS YOU WANT AND YOU NEVER HAVE TO COME WHEN THEY CALL YOU.
© 1994 Grimmy Inc. Distributed By Tribune Media Services

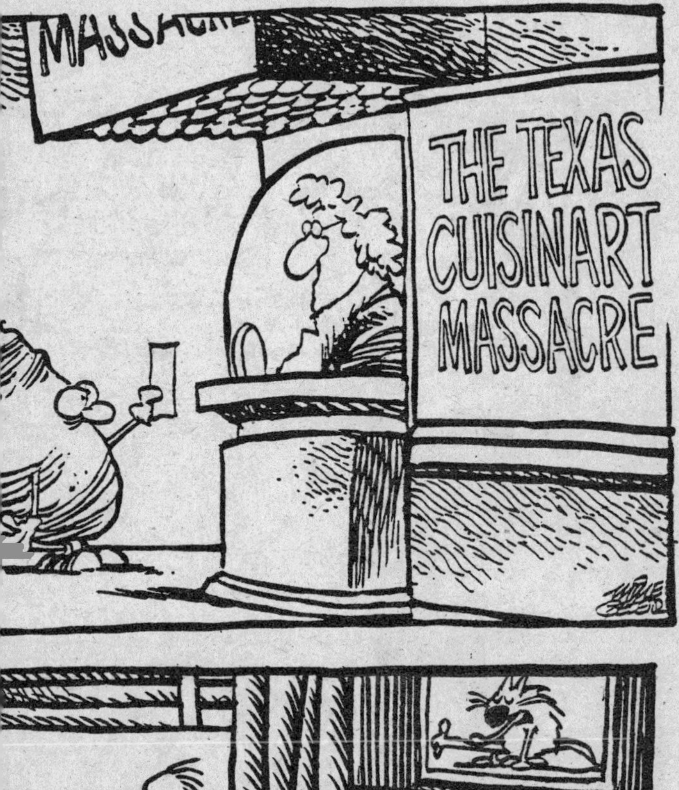
THE TEXAS
CUISINART
MASSACRE

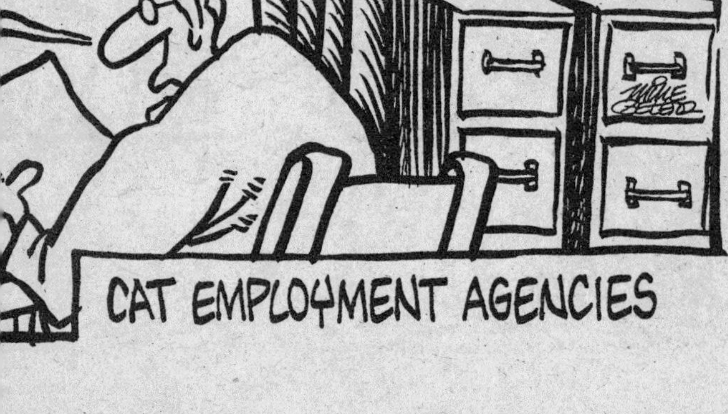

CAT EMPLOYMENT AGENCIES

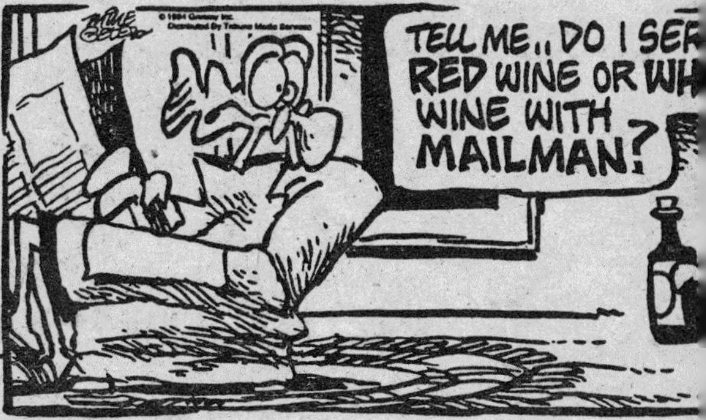
TELL ME.. DO I SER
RED WINE OR WH
WINE WITH
MAILMAN?

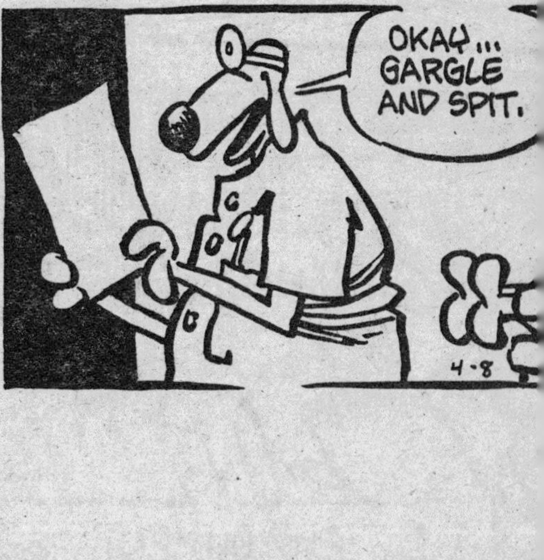
OKAY...
GARGLE
AND SPIT.
4-8

4-5
I LIKE THIS GUY.
DOG DENTISTS

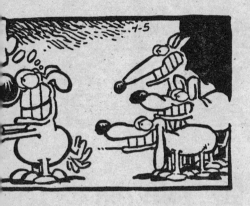

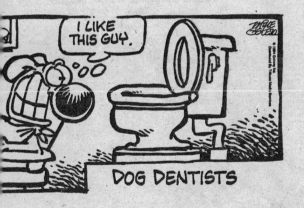

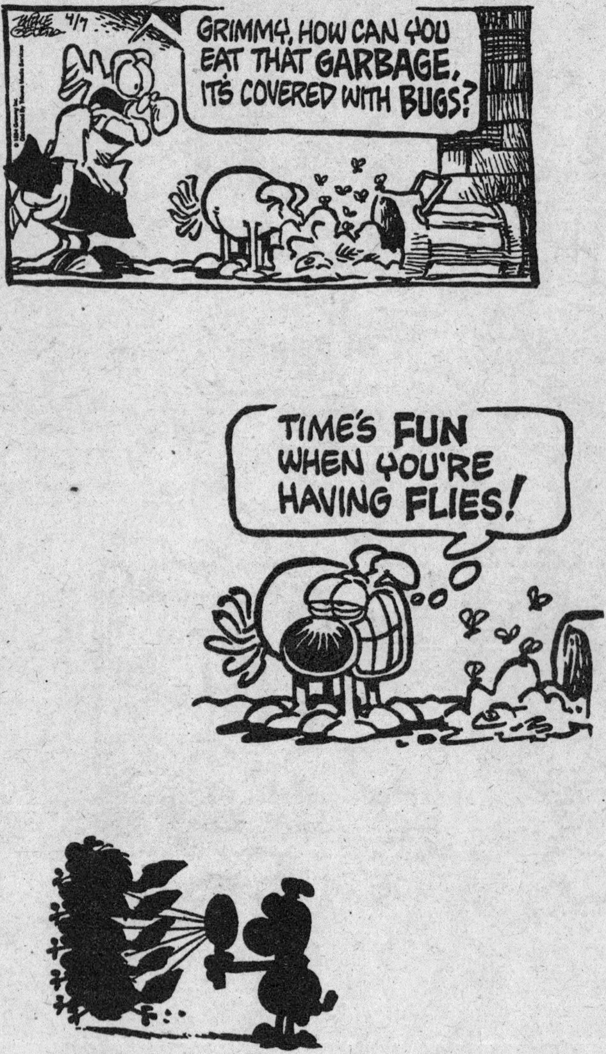
4/7
GRIMMY, HOW CAN YOU EAT THAT GARBAGE, IT'S COVERED WITH BUGS?
TIME'S FUN WHEN YOU'RE HAVING FLIES!

LOOK AT THIS MESS! I FEED YOU, I GIVE YOU SHELTER AND WHAT DO YOU GIVE ME?
HIGH BLOOD PRESSURE.
4-9

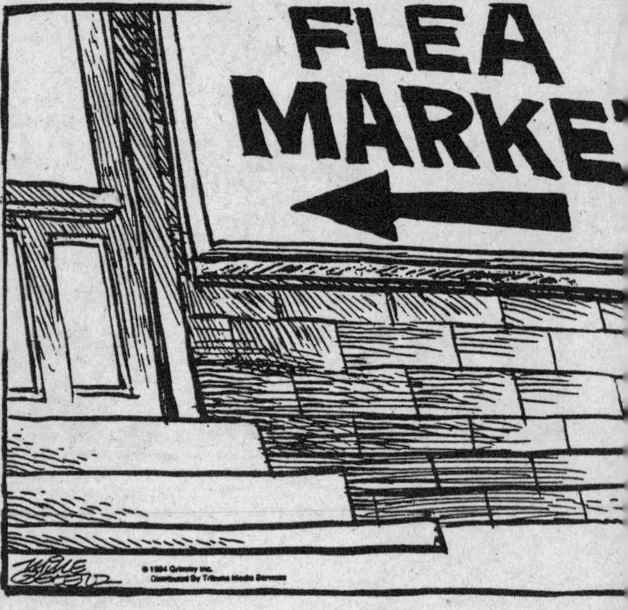
FLEA
MARKE
© 1994 Grimmy Inc.
Distributed By Tribune Media Services

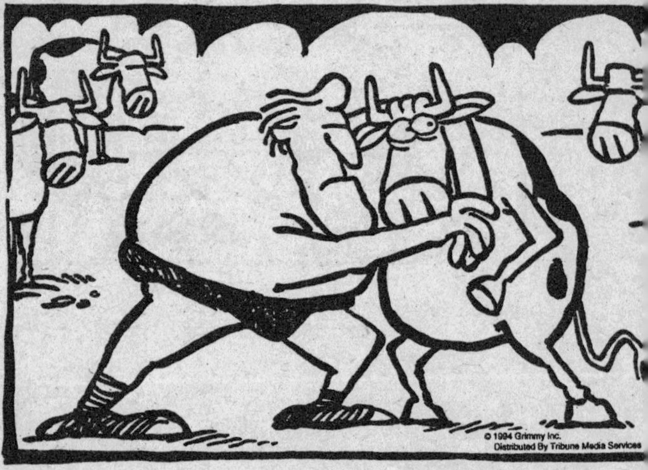
© 1994 Grimmy Inc.
Distributed By Tribune Media Services

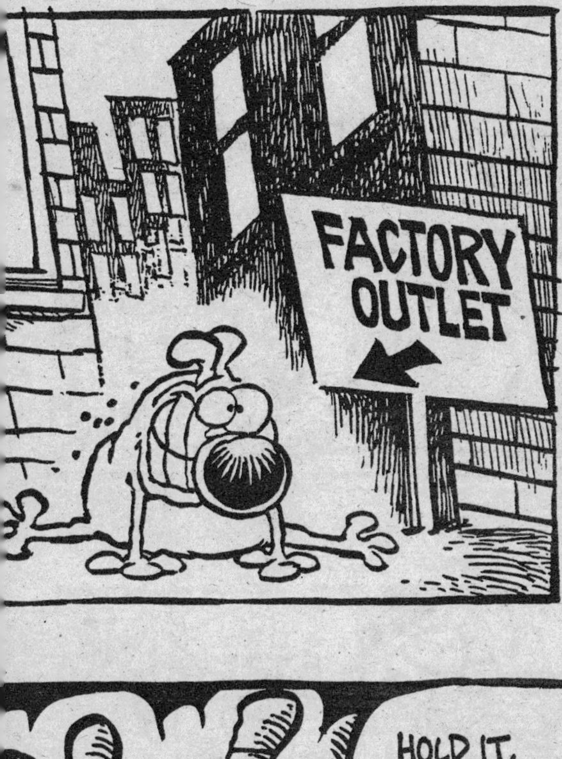
FACTORY
OUTLET

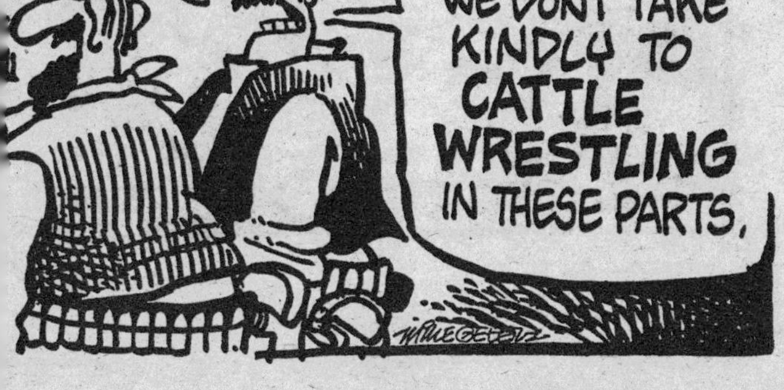
HOLD IT, STRANGER.... WE DON'T TAKE KINDLY TO CATTLE WRESTLING IN THESE PARTS.
MIKE GEERTZ

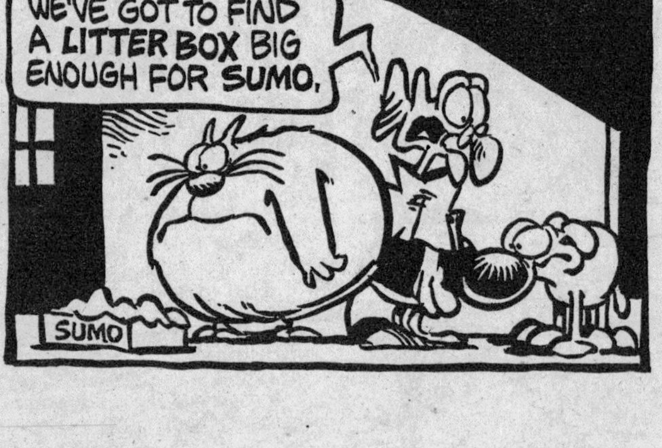
WE'VE GOT TO FIND A LITTER BOX BIG ENOUGH FOR SUMO.
SUMO

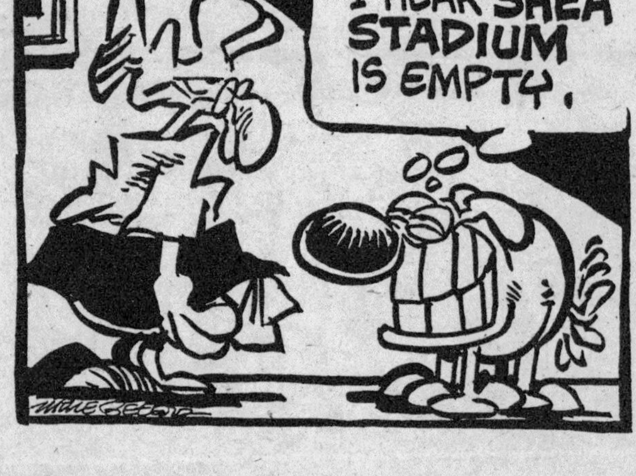
I HEAR SHEA STADIUM IS EMPTY.

OKAY, ATTILA, YOU CAN HAVE SOME OF MY FOOD.
GRIMMY, WHAT A SWEET THING TO DO...
4-19
SORRY, THAT WAS A RANDOM ACT OF SENSELESS KINDNESS.

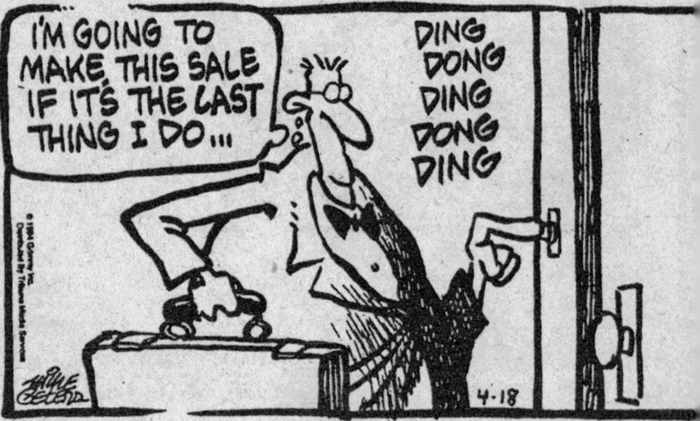
I'M GOING TO MAKE THIS SALE IF IT'S THE LAST THING I DO...
DING DONG DING DONG DING
4-18

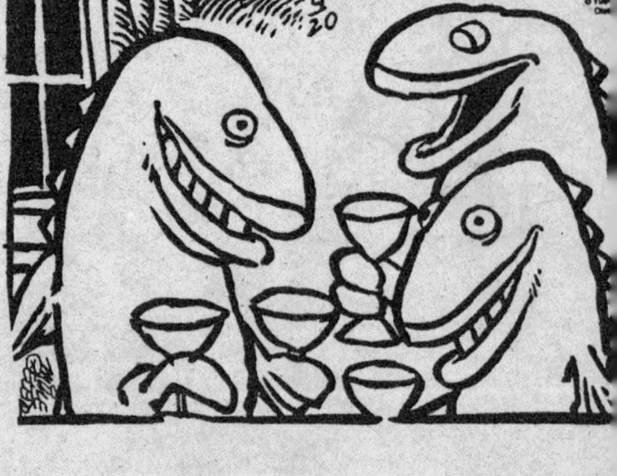
4/20

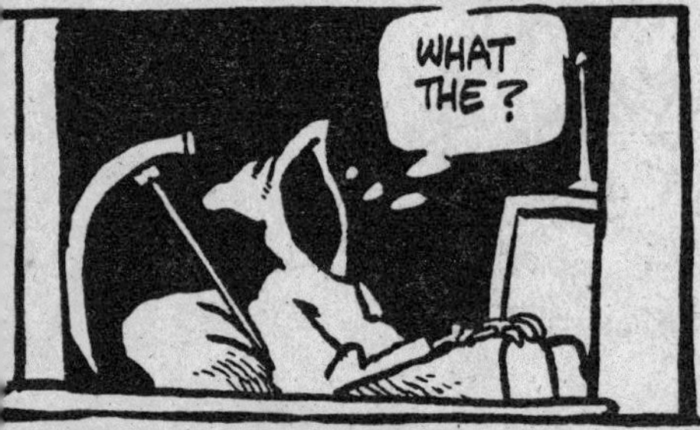
WHAT THE ?

ERB LEARNED TOO LATE HE
WAS AT DEATH'S DOOR

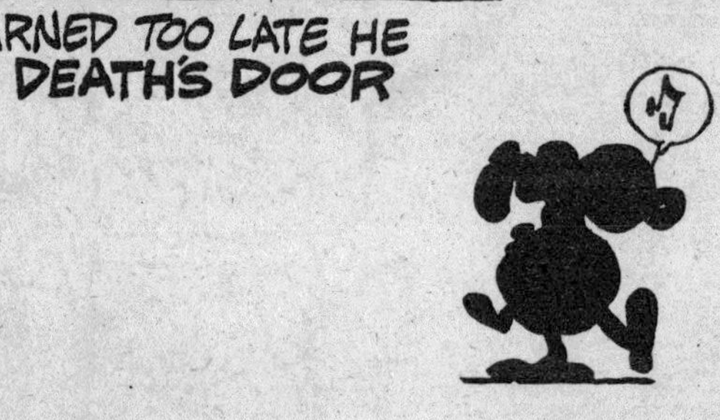

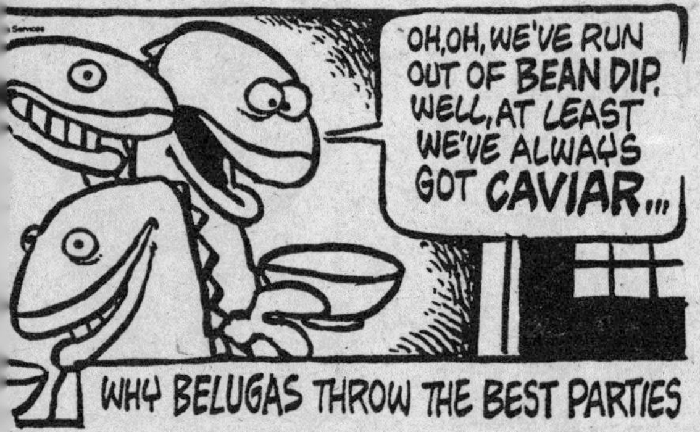
OH, OH, WE'VE RUN OUT OF BEAN DIP. WELL, AT LEAST WE'VE ALWAYS GOT CAVIAR...

WHY BELUGAS THROW THE BEST PARTIES

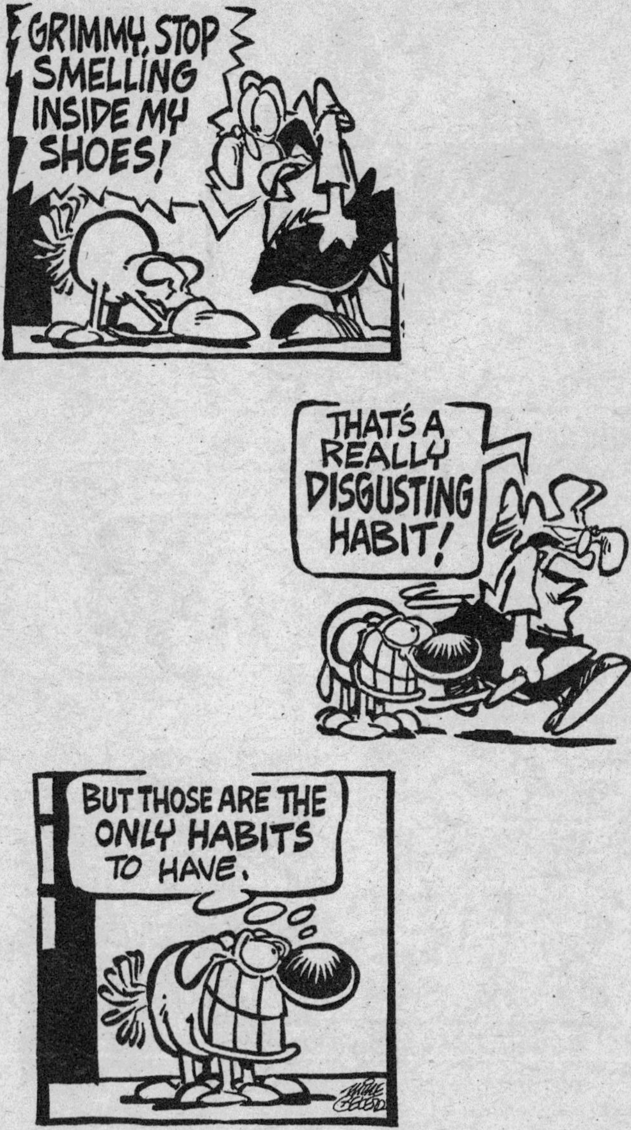
GRIMMY, STOP SMELLING INSIDE MY SHOES!
THAT'S A REALLY DISGUSTING HABIT!
BUT THOSE ARE THE ONLY HABITS TO HAVE.

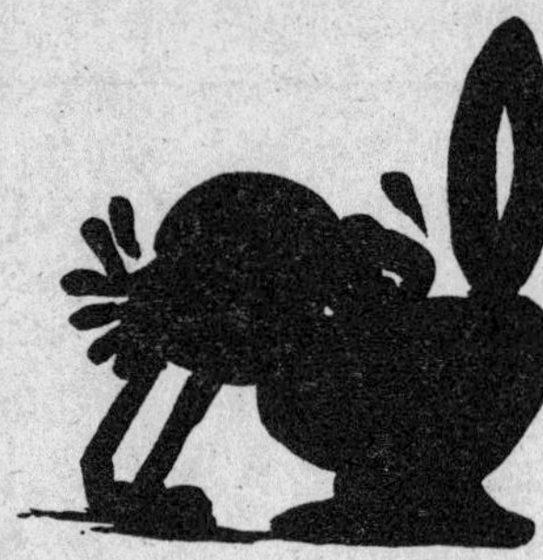

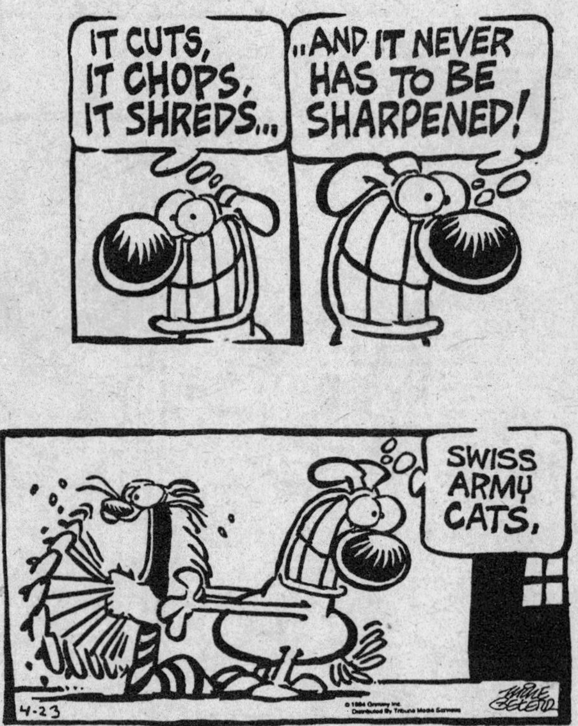

IT CUTS, IT CHOPS, IT SHREDS...
..AND IT NEVER HAS TO BE SHARPENED!
SWISS ARMY CATS.
4-23

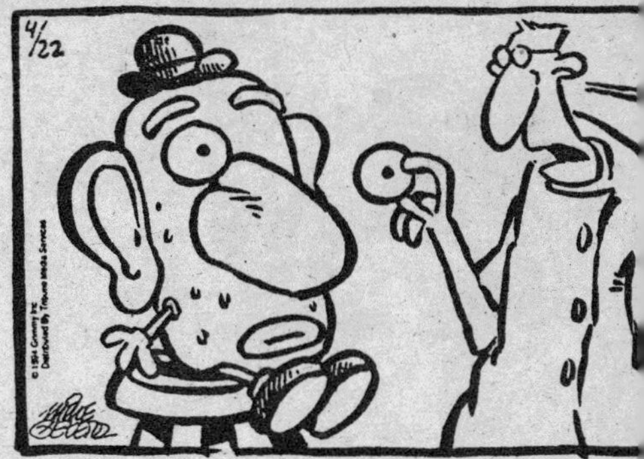
4/22

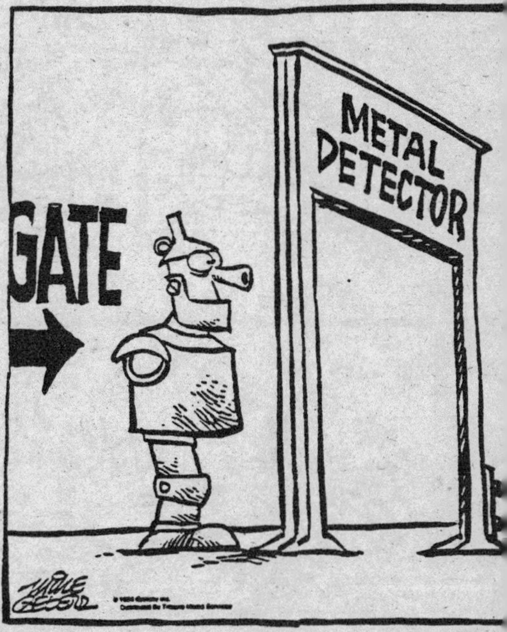
METAL DETECTOR
GATE

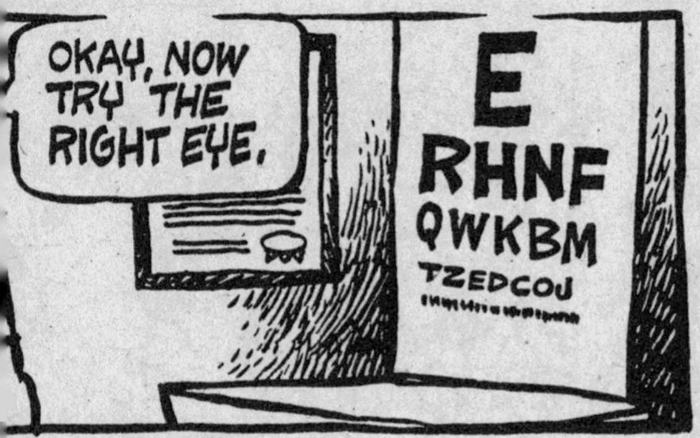
OKAY, NOW TRY THE RIGHT EYE.
E
RHNF
QWKBM
TZEDCOJ

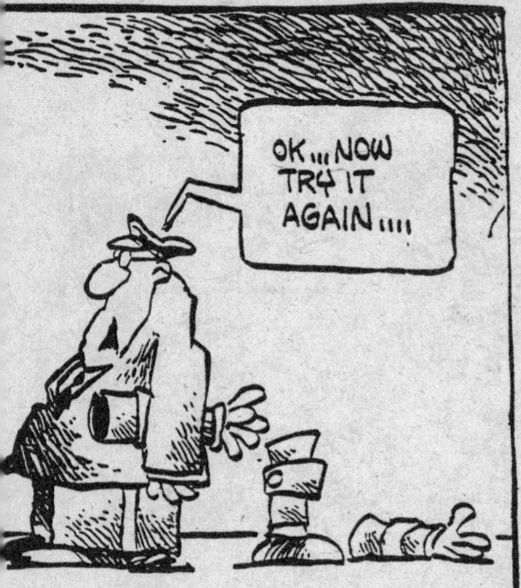
OK... NOW TRY IT AGAIN....

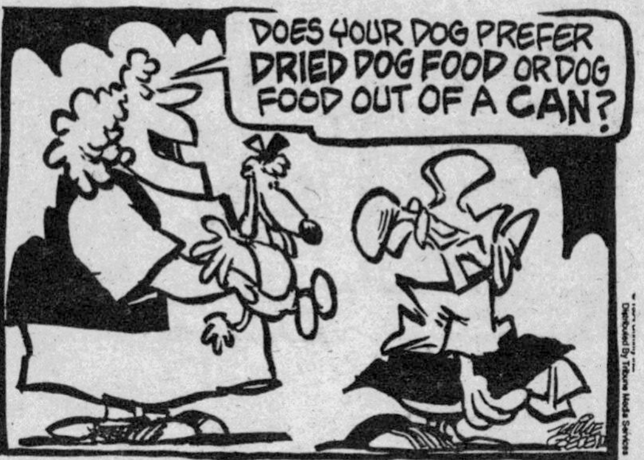
DOES YOUR DOG PREFER DRIED DOG FOOD OR DOG FOOD OUT OF A CAN?
Distributed By Tribune Media Services

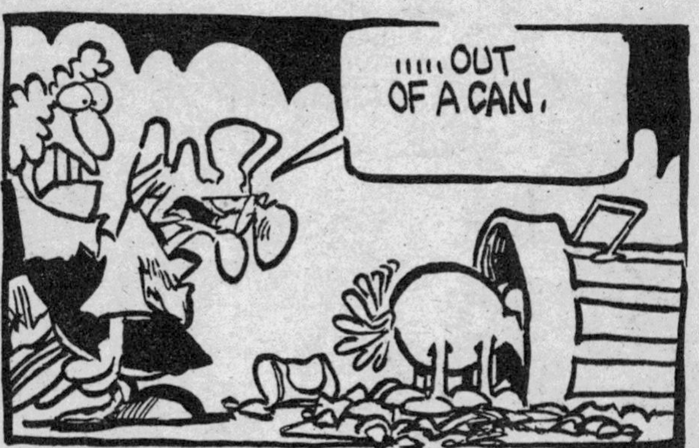
..... OUT OF A CAN.

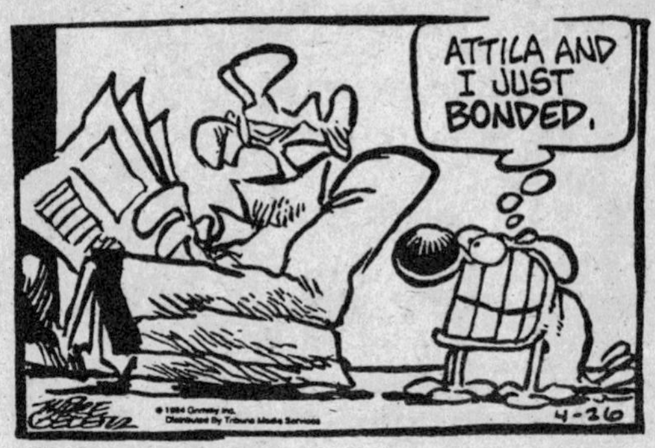
ATTILA AND I JUST BONDED.
Distributed By Tribune Media Services
4-26

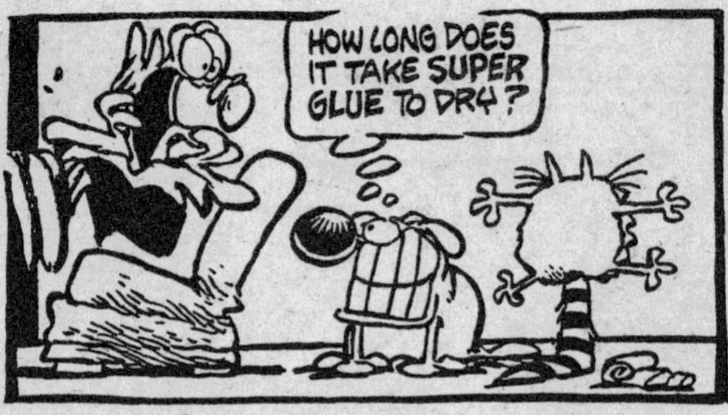
HOW LONG DOES IT TAKE SUPER GLUE TO DRY?

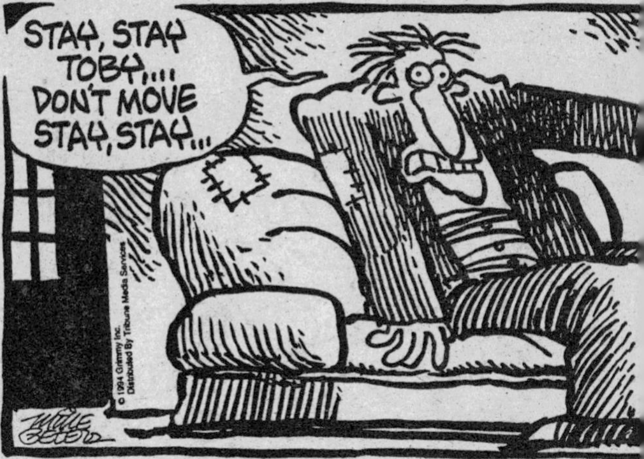
STAY, STAY TOBY,... DON'T MOVE STAY, STAY...
© 1994 Grimmy Inc. Distributed By Tribune Media Services
MIKE PETERS

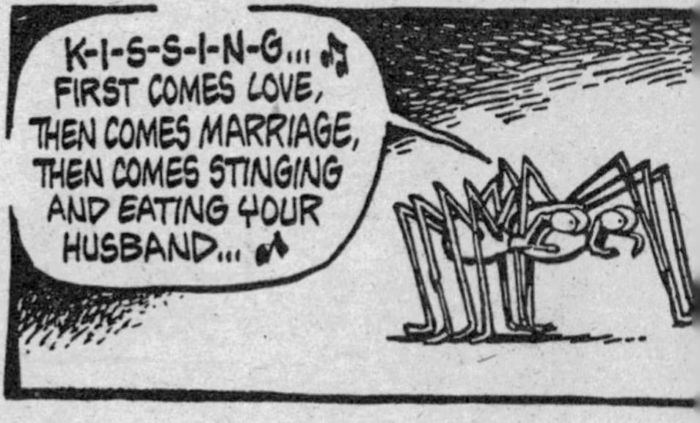
K-I-S-S-I-N-G... FIRST COMES LOVE, THEN COMES MARRIAGE, THEN COMES STINGING AND EATING YOUR HUSBAND...

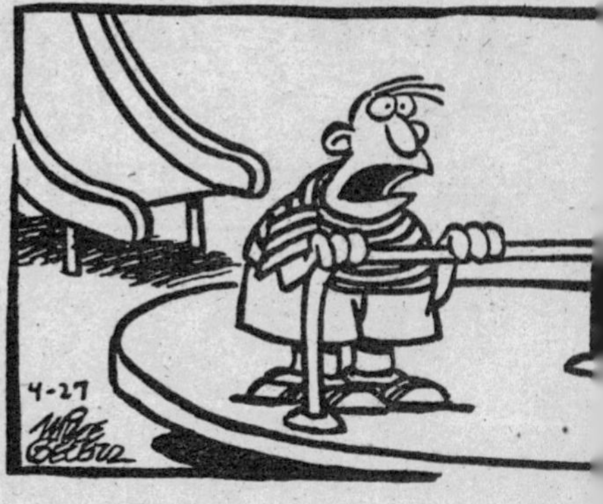
4-27
MIKE PETERS

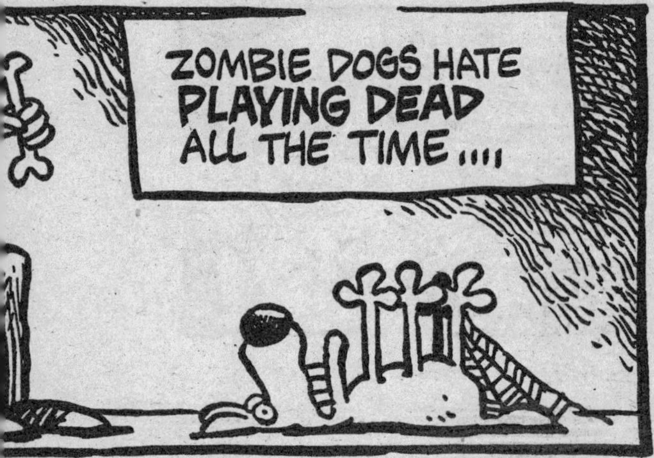
ZOMBIE DOGS HATE PLAYING DEAD ALL THE TIME....

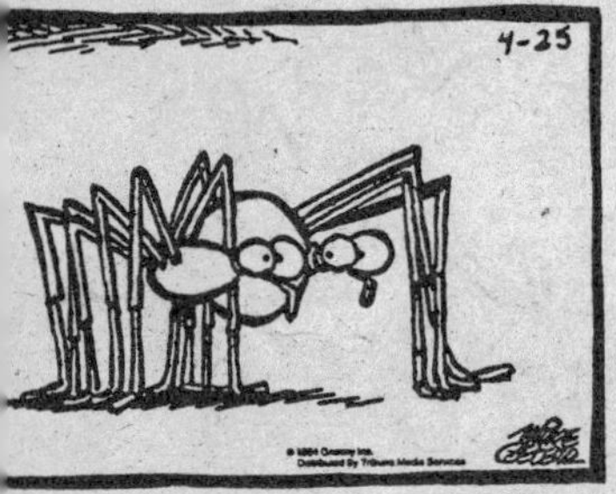
4-25

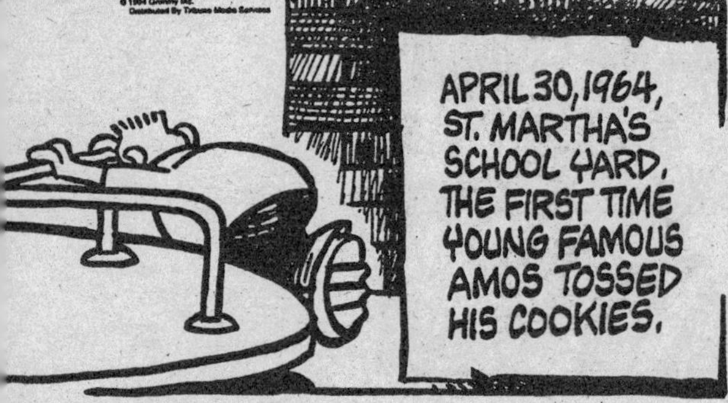
APRIL 30, 1964, ST. MARTHA'S SCHOOL YARD. THE FIRST TIME YOUNG FAMOUS AMOS TOSSED HIS COOKIES.

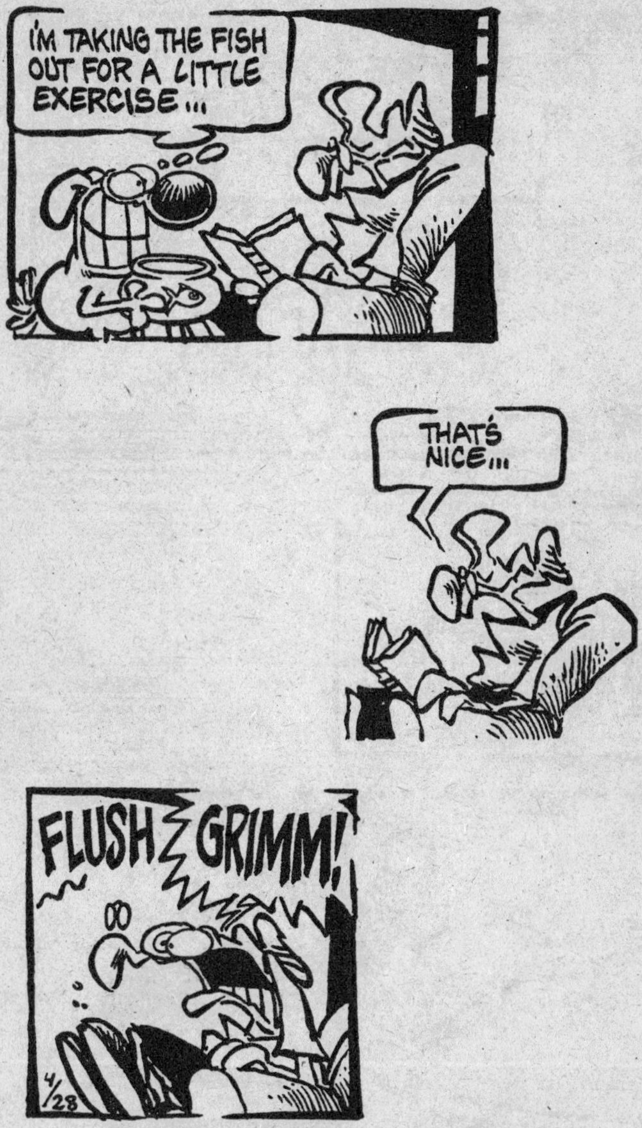
I'M TAKING THE FISH OUT FOR A LITTLE EXERCISE...
THAT'S NICE...
FLUSH
GRIMM!
4/28

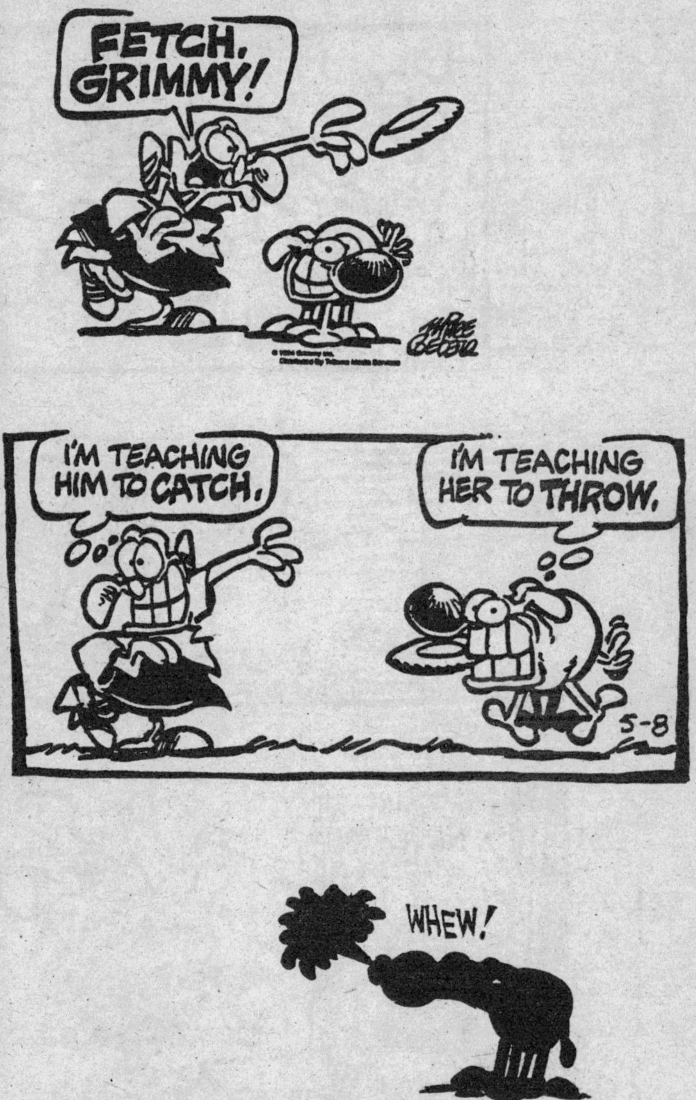
FETCH, GRIMMY!
I'M TEACHING HIM TO CATCH.
I'M TEACHING HER TO THROW.
5-8
WHEW!

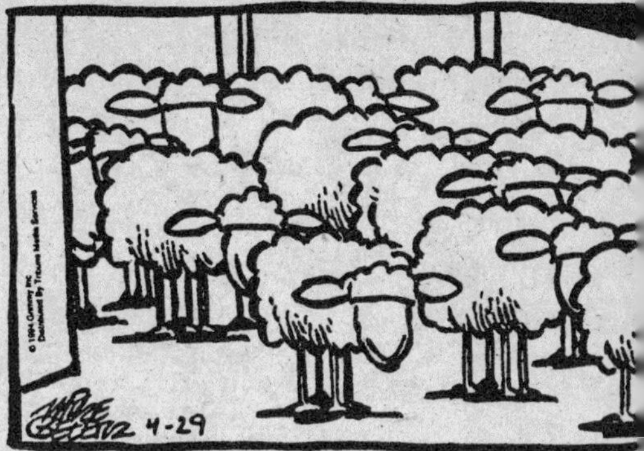
4-29

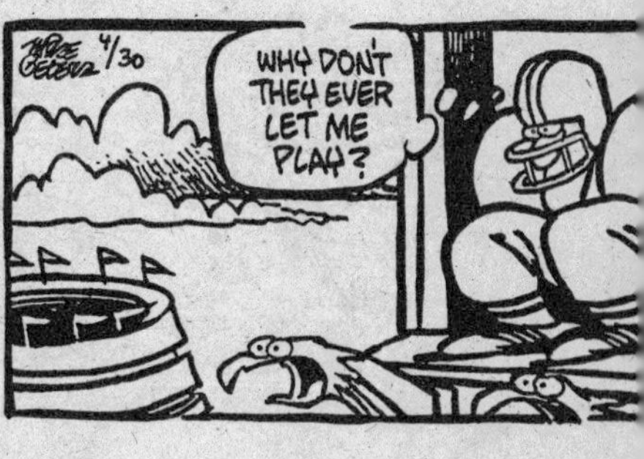
4/30
WHY DON'T THEY EVER LET ME PLAY?

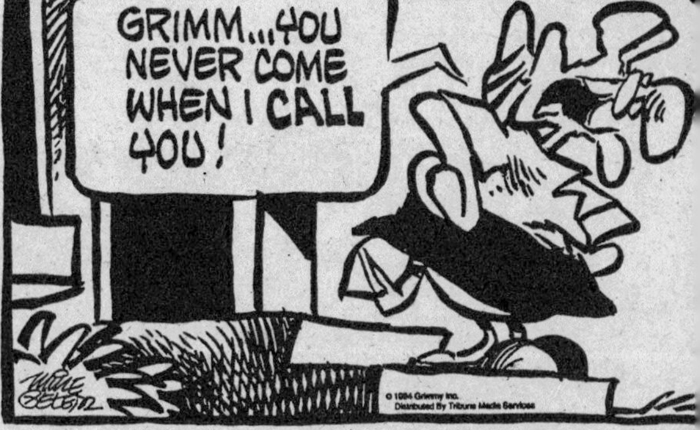
GRIMM...YOU NEVER COME WHEN I CALL YOU!
© 1994 Grimmy Inc. Distributed By Tribune Media Services

THAT'S THE LAST TIME I O WALKING WITH A BORDER COLLIE.

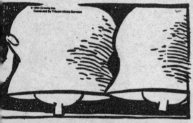

THE QUARTERBACK OF NOTRE DAME

YOU NEVER CALL ME ON MY **PRIVATE** NUMBER.

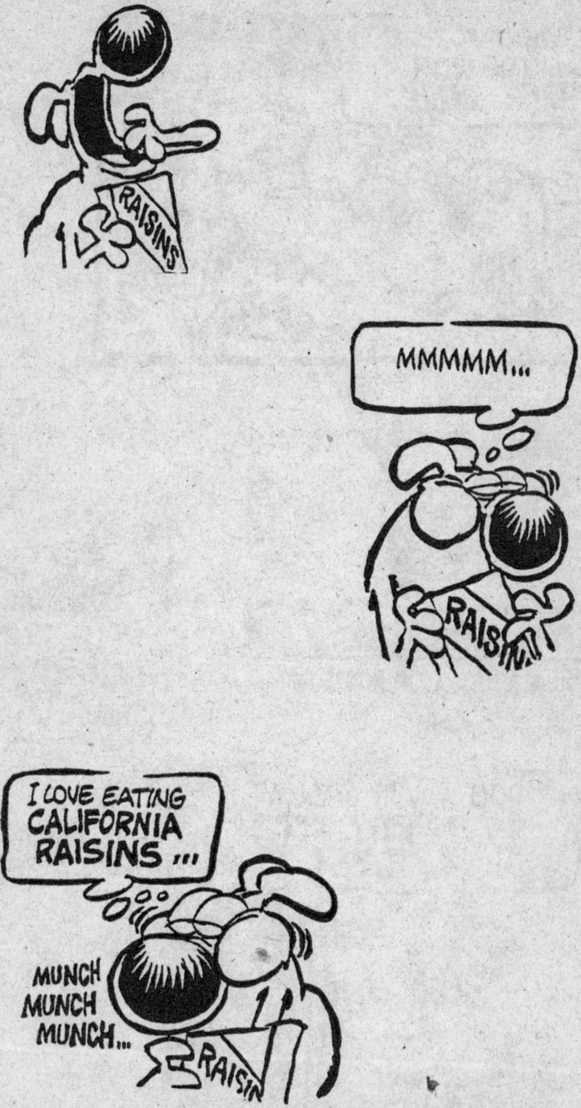
RAISINS
MMMMM...
RAISIN
I LOVE EATING CALIFORNIA RAISINS ...
MUNCH MUNCH MUNCH...
RAISIN

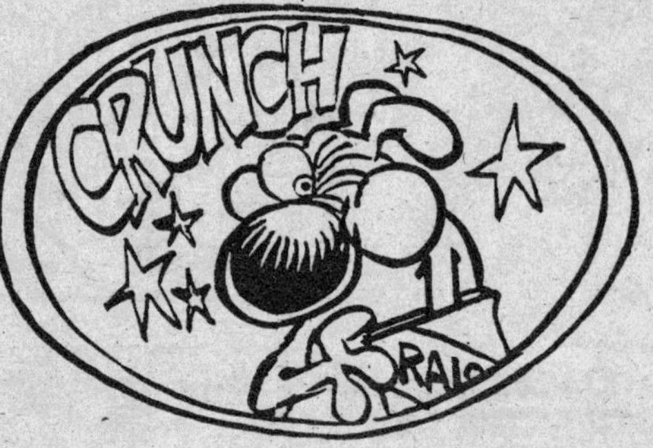
CRUNCH

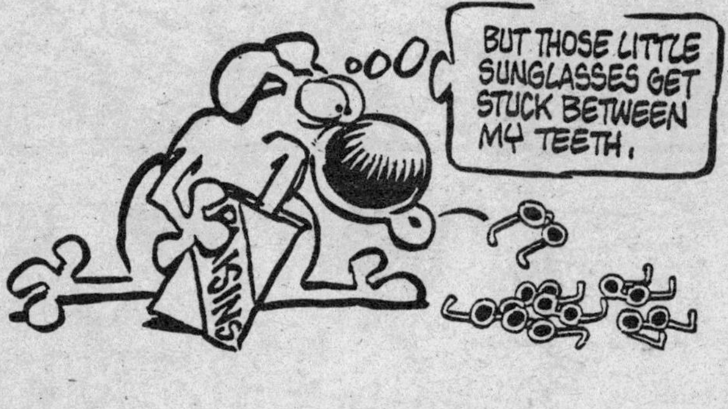
OOO
BUT THOSE LITTLE SUNGLASSES GET STUCK BETWEEN MY TEETH.
RAISINS

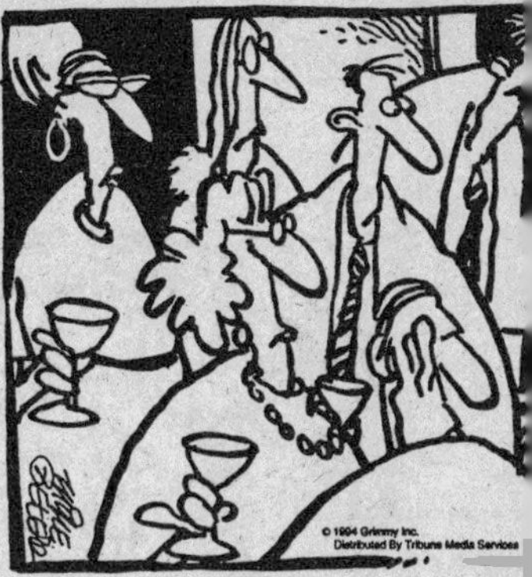
© 1994 Grimmy Inc.
Distributed By Tribune Media Services

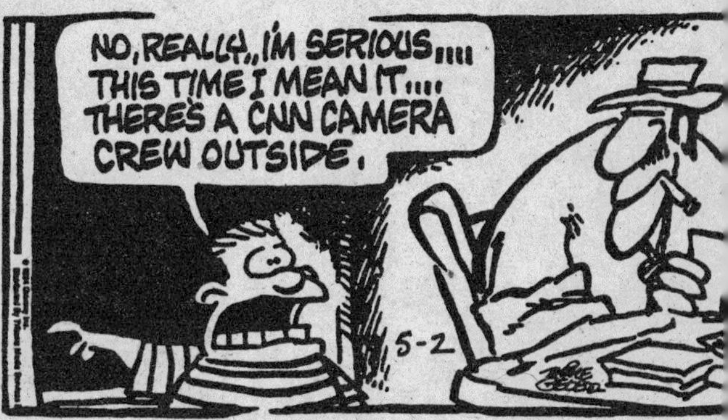
NO, REALLY.. I'M SERIOUS.... THIS TIME I MEAN IT.... THERE'S A CNN CAMERA CREW OUTSIDE.
5-2

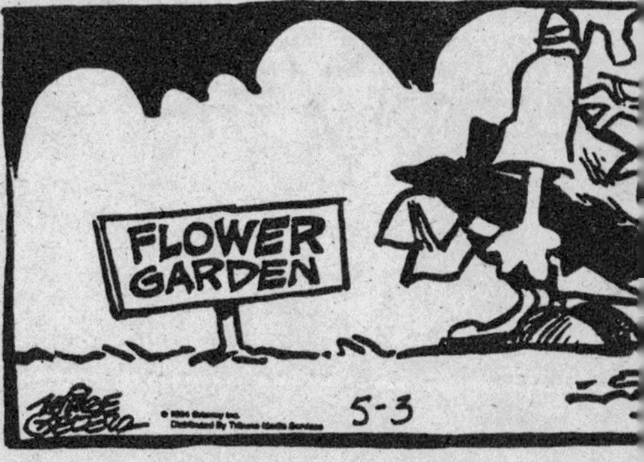
FLOWER GARDEN
5-3

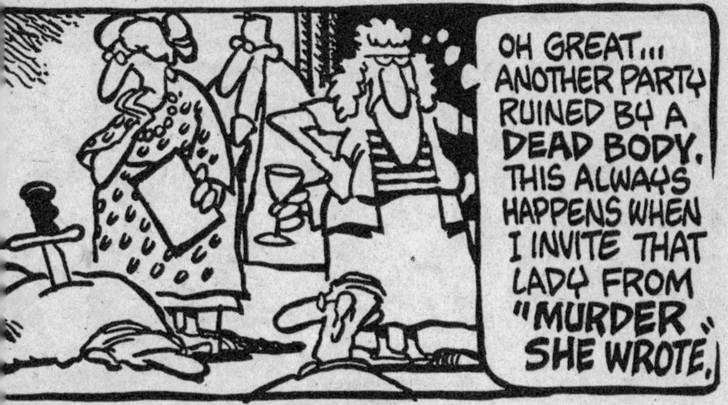
OH GREAT... ANOTHER PARTY RUINED BY A DEAD BODY. THIS ALWAYS HAPPENS WHEN I INVITE THAT LADY FROM "MURDER SHE WROTE."

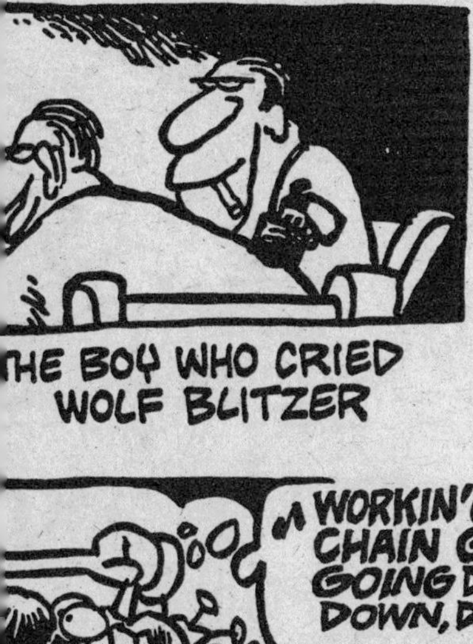

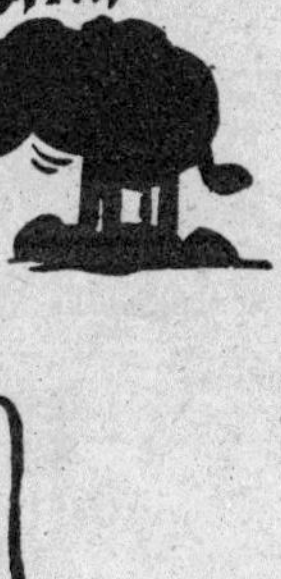
BELCH...

THE BOY WHO CRIED WOLF BLITZER

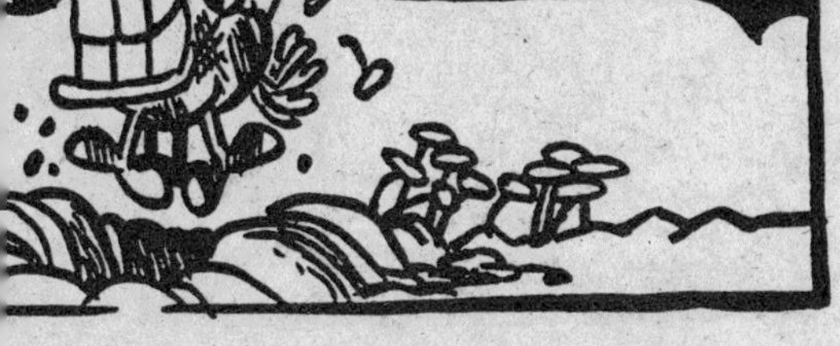
♪ WORKIN' ON THE CHAIN GANG, GOING DOWN, DOWN, DOWN, DOWN. ♪

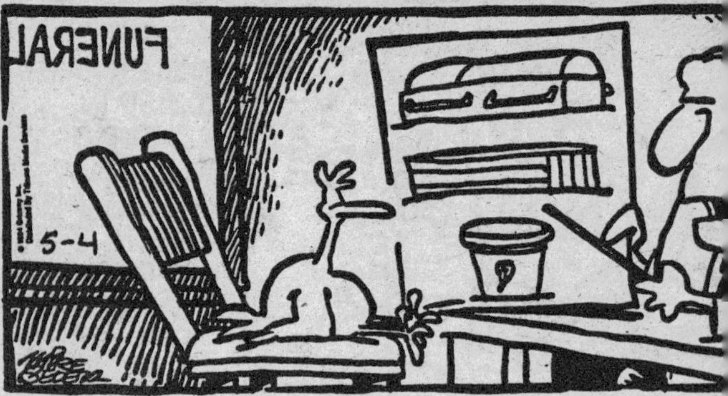
FUNERAL
5-4

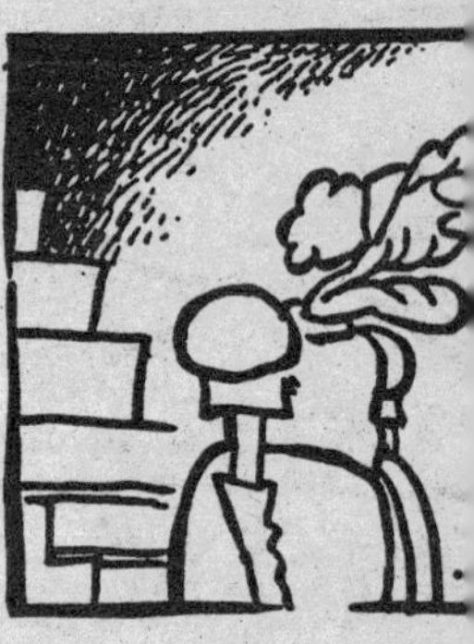

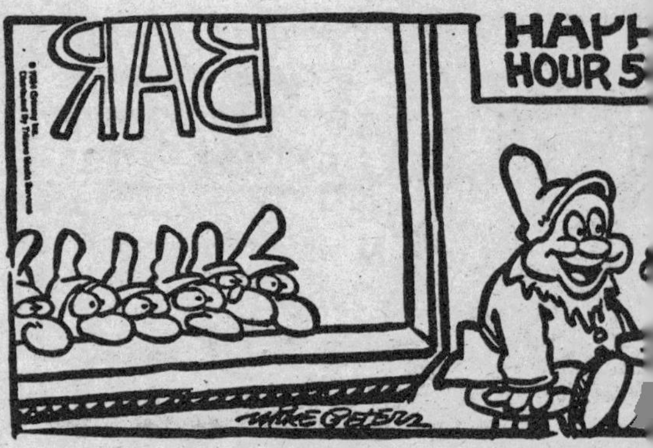
BAR
HAPP
HOUR 5

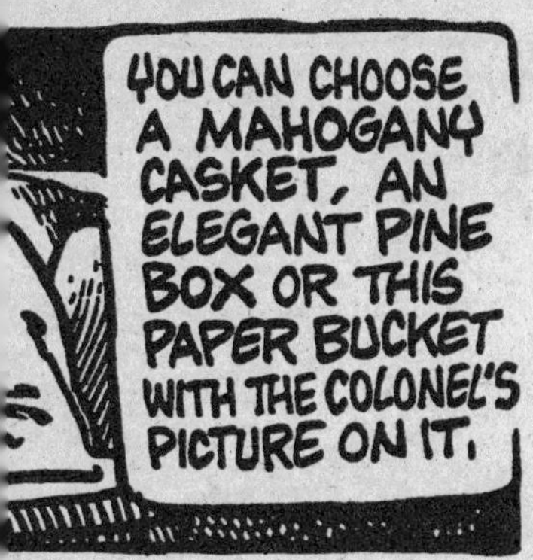
YOU CAN CHOOSE A MAHOGANY CASKET, AN ELEGANT PINE BOX OR THIS PAPER BUCKET WITH THE COLONEL'S PICTURE ON IT.

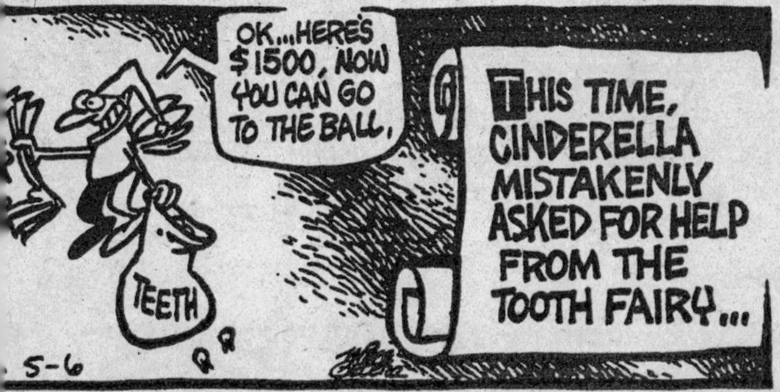
THIS TIME, CINDERELLA MISTAKENLY ASKED FOR HELP FROM THE TOOTH FAIRY...
OK...HERE'S $1500, NOW YOU CAN GO TO THE BALL.
TEETH
5-6

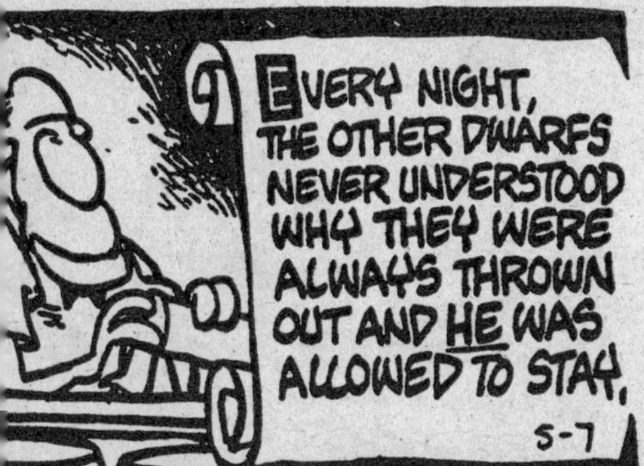
EVERY NIGHT, THE OTHER DWARFS NEVER UNDERSTOOD WHY THEY WERE ALWAYS THROWN OUT AND HE WAS ALLOWED TO STAY.
5-7

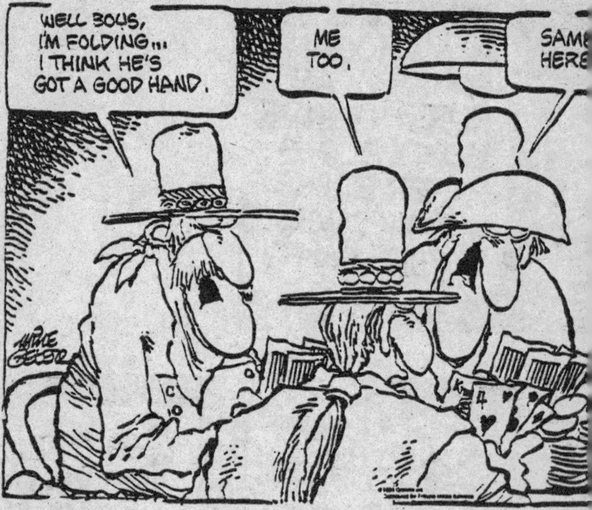
WELL BOYS, I'M FOLDING... I THINK HE'S GOT A GOOD HAND.
ME TOO.
SAM
HER

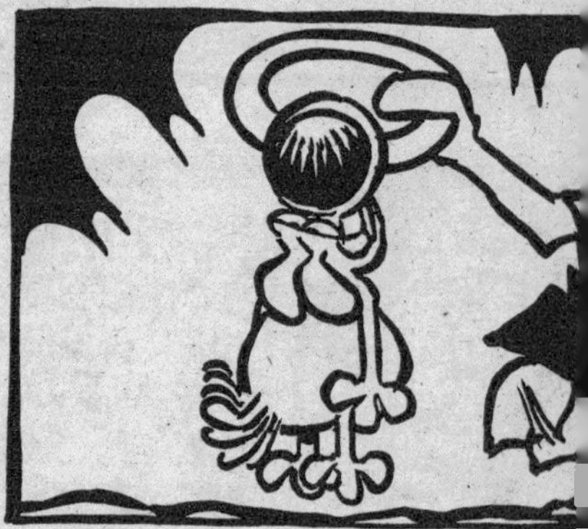

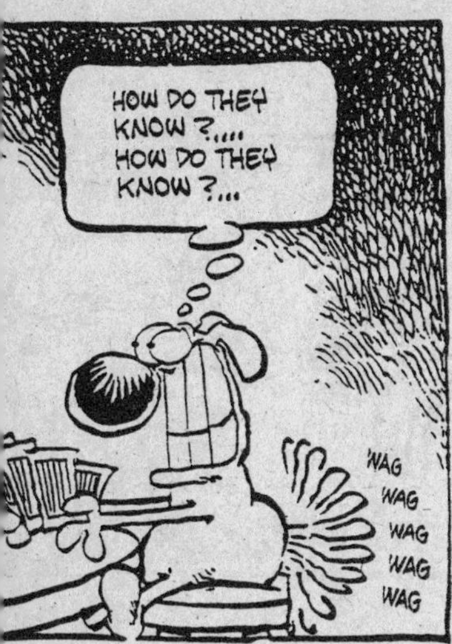
HOW DO THEY KNOW ?..... HOW DO THEY KNOW ?...
WAG
WAG
WAG
WAG
WAG

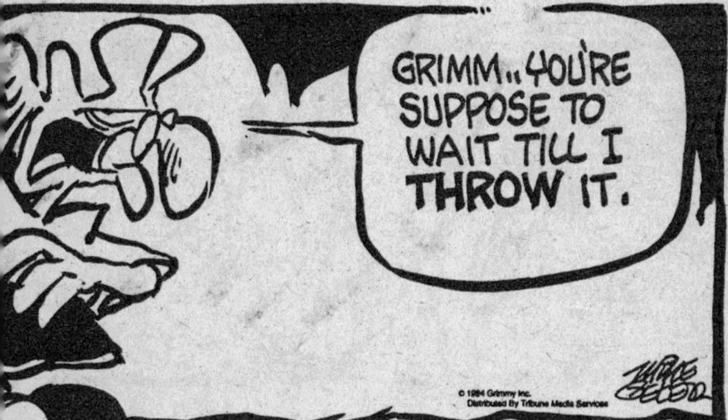
GRIMM.. YOU'RE SUPPOSE TO WAIT TILL I THROW IT.
© 1994 Grimmy Inc.
Distributed By Tribune Media Services

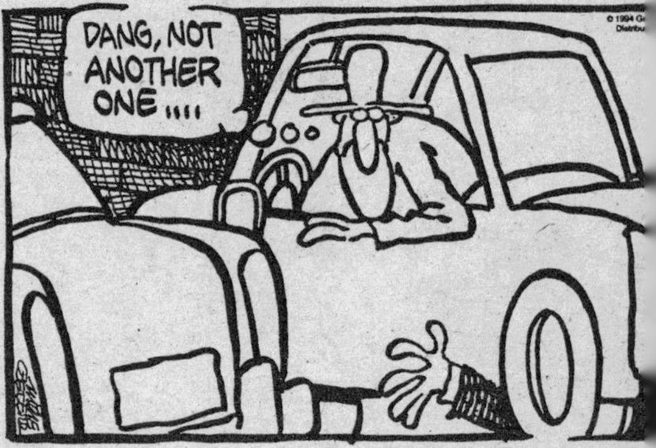
DANG, NOT ANOTHER ONE....

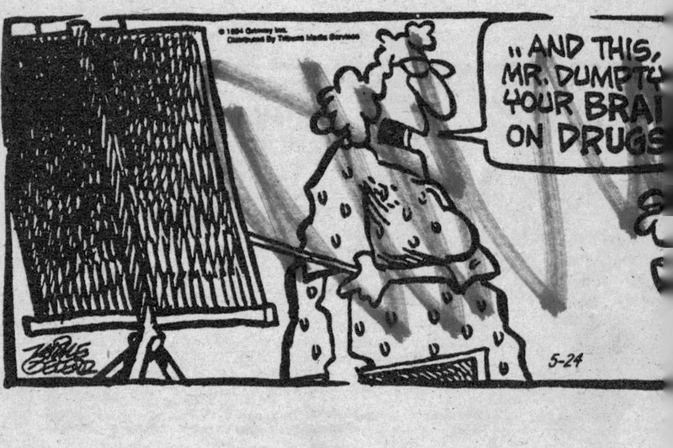
.. AND THIS,
MR. DUMPTY
YOUR BRAI
ON DRUGS
5-24

VAMPIRES ARE NOT VISIBLE IN MIRRORS, WHICH EXPLAINS WHY THEY ARE OFTEN BACKED-OVER IN PARKING LOTS.

WHY HUMPTY HATED HEALTH CLASS...

MY DOG JUST WON BEST IN SHOW.
5-23
MY DOG JUST WON BEST IN CHEW AND SHOW.

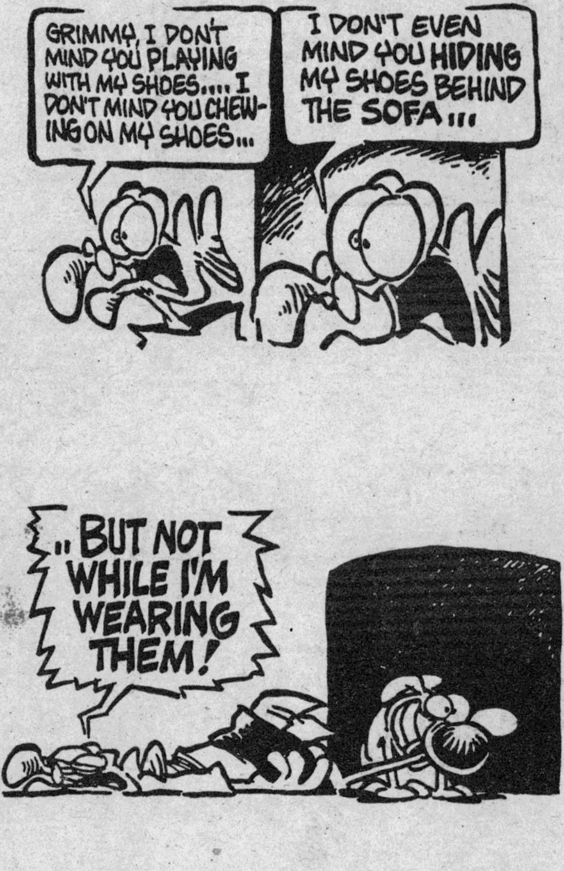
GRIMMY, I DON'T MIND YOU PLAYING WITH MY SHOES.... I DON'T MIND YOU CHEWING ON MY SHOES...
I DON'T EVEN MIND YOU HIDING MY SHOES BEHIND THE SOFA...
.. BUT NOT WHILE I'M WEARING THEM!

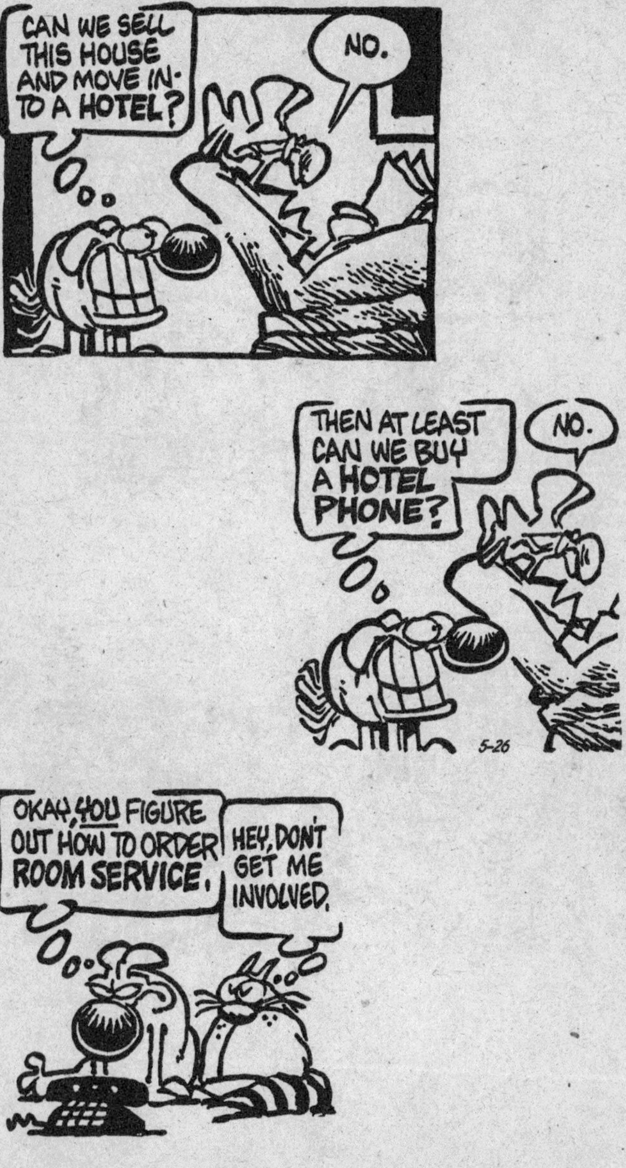

CAN WE SELL THIS HOUSE AND MOVE INTO A HOTEL?
NO.
THEN AT LEAST CAN WE BUY A HOTEL PHONE?
NO.
5-26
OKAY, YOU FIGURE OUT HOW TO ORDER ROOM SERVICE.
HEY, DON'T GET ME INVOLVED.

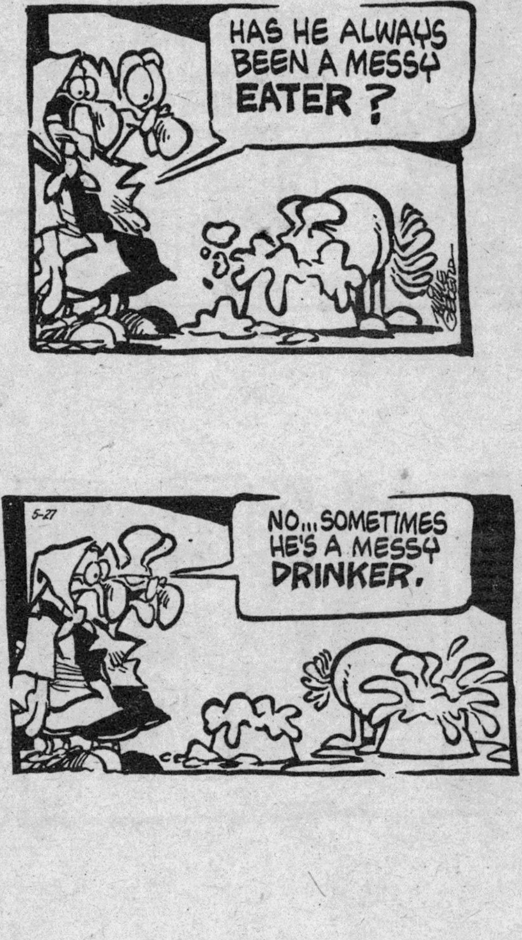
HAS HE ALWAYS BEEN A MESSY EATER?
5-27
NO... SOMETIMES HE'S A MESSY DRINKER.

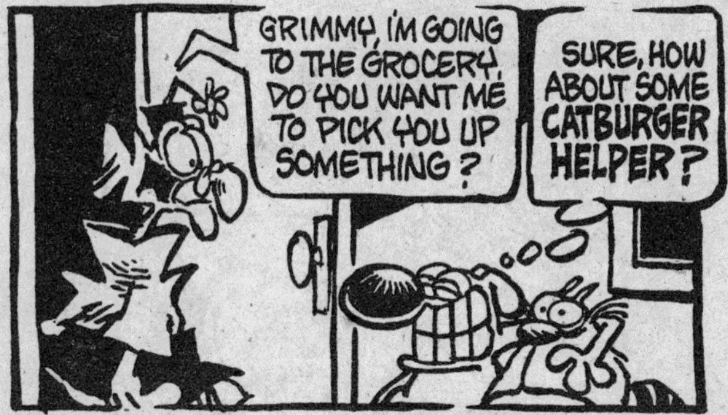
GRIMMY, I'M GOING TO THE GROCERY. DO YOU WANT ME TO PICK YOU UP SOMETHING?
SURE, HOW ABOUT SOME CATBURGER HELPER?

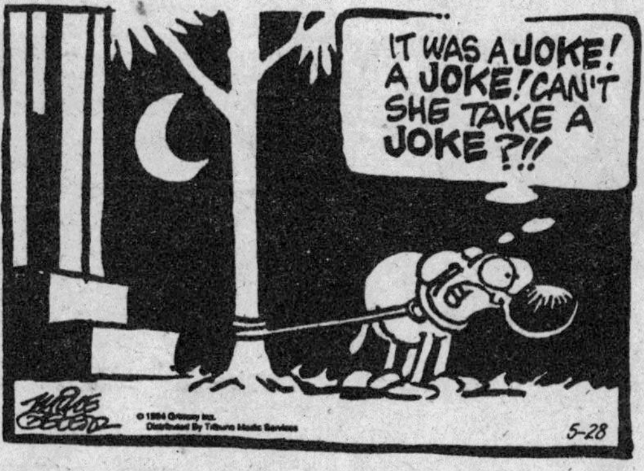
IT WAS A JOKE! A JOKE! CAN'T SHE TAKE A JOKE?!!
Distributed By Tribune Media Services
5-28

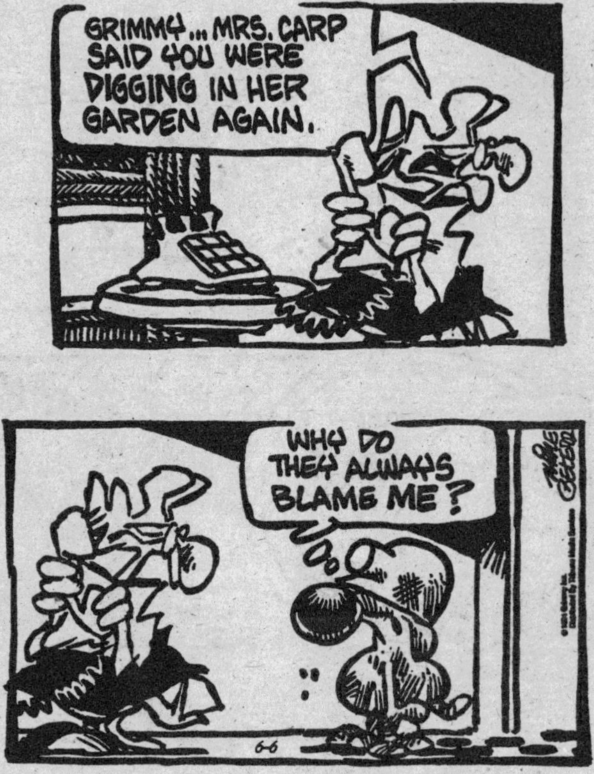
GRIMMY... MRS. CARP SAID YOU WERE DIGGING IN HER GARDEN AGAIN.
WHY DO THEY ALWAYS BLAME ME?
6-6

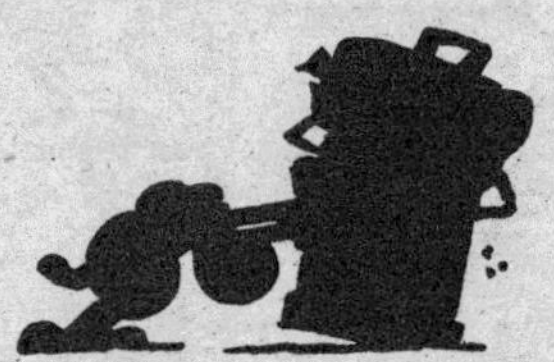

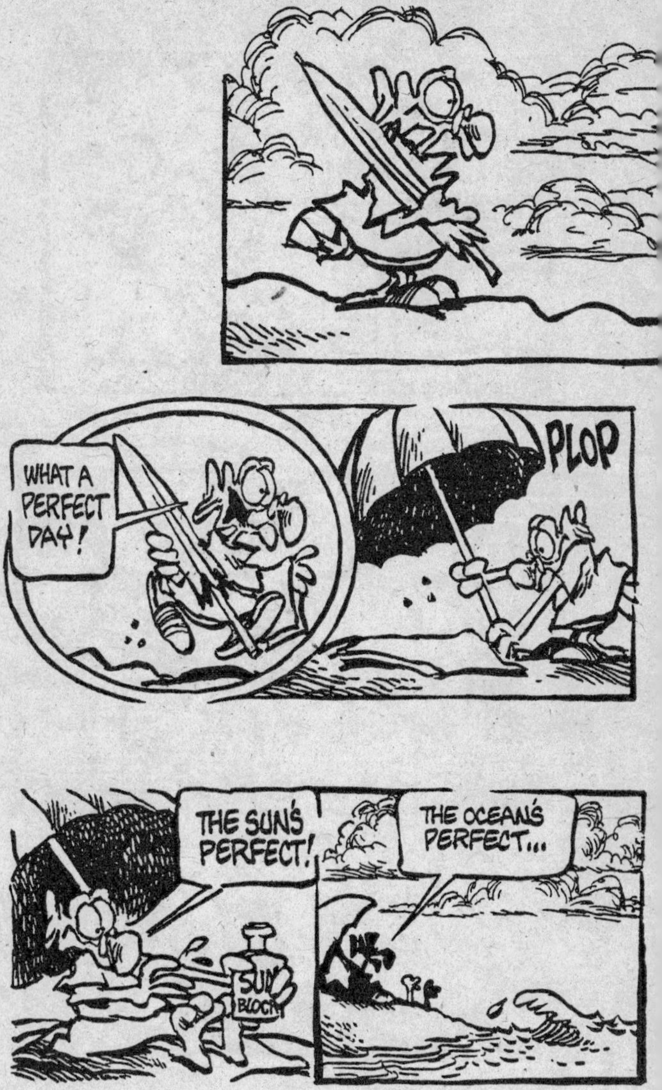
WHAT A PERFECT DAY!
PLOP
THE SUN'S PERFECT!
SUN BLOCK
THE OCEAN'S PERFECT...

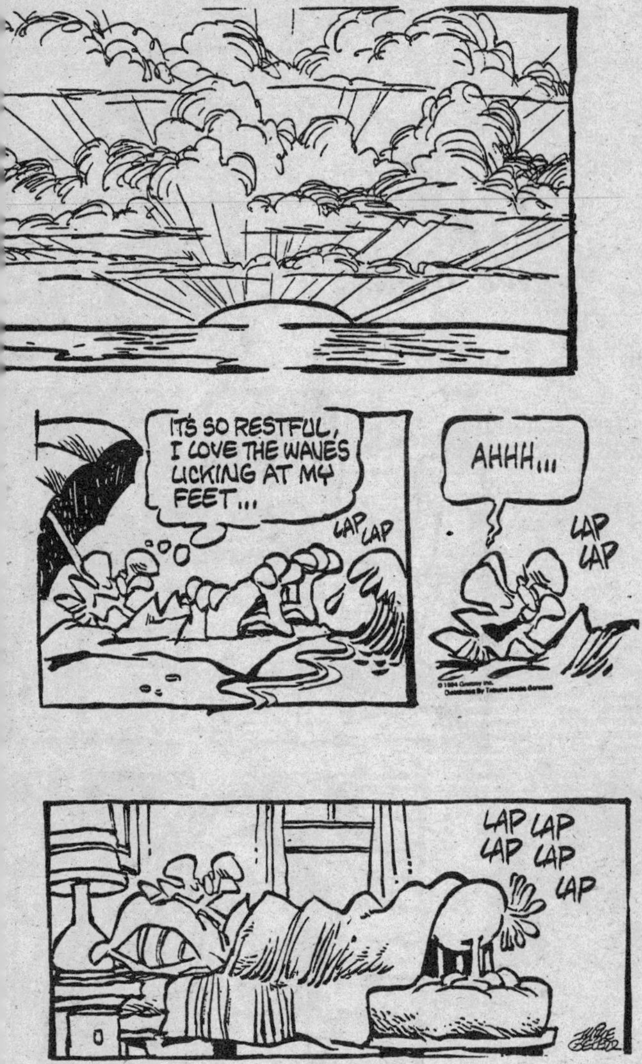

IT'S SO RESTFUL, I LOVE THE WAVES LICKING AT MY FEET...
LAP LAP
AHHH...
LAP LAP
LAP LAP LAP LAP LAP

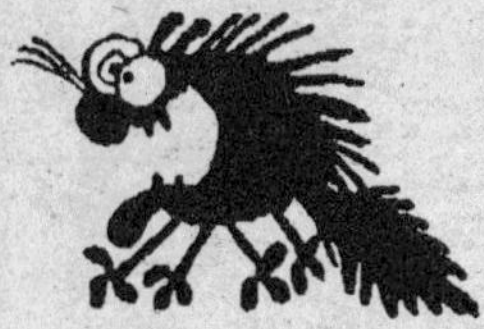

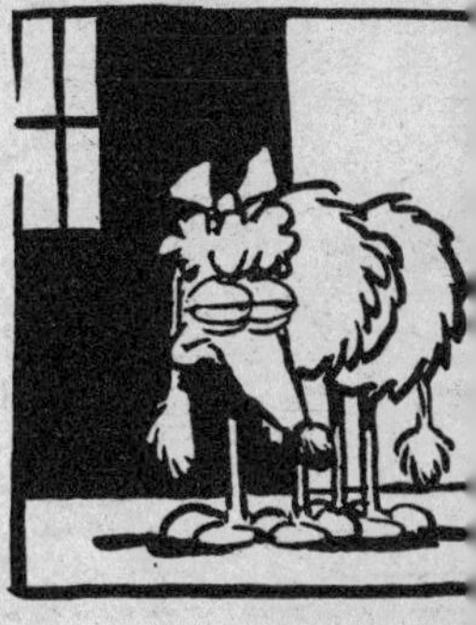

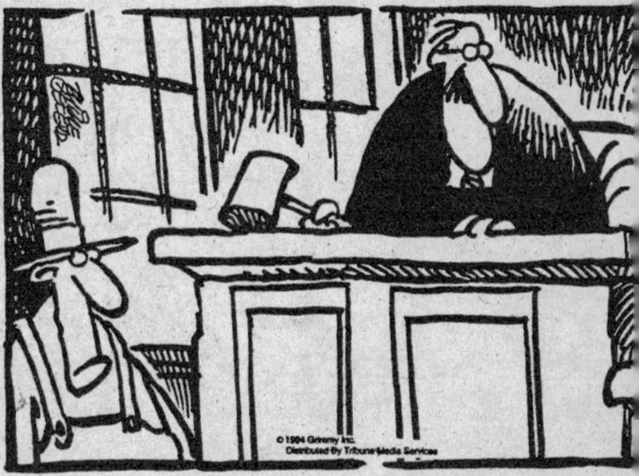
© 1984 Grimmy Inc.
Distributed By Tribune Media Services

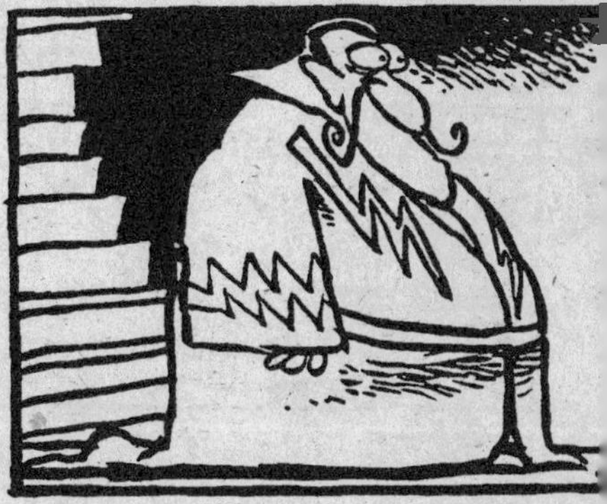

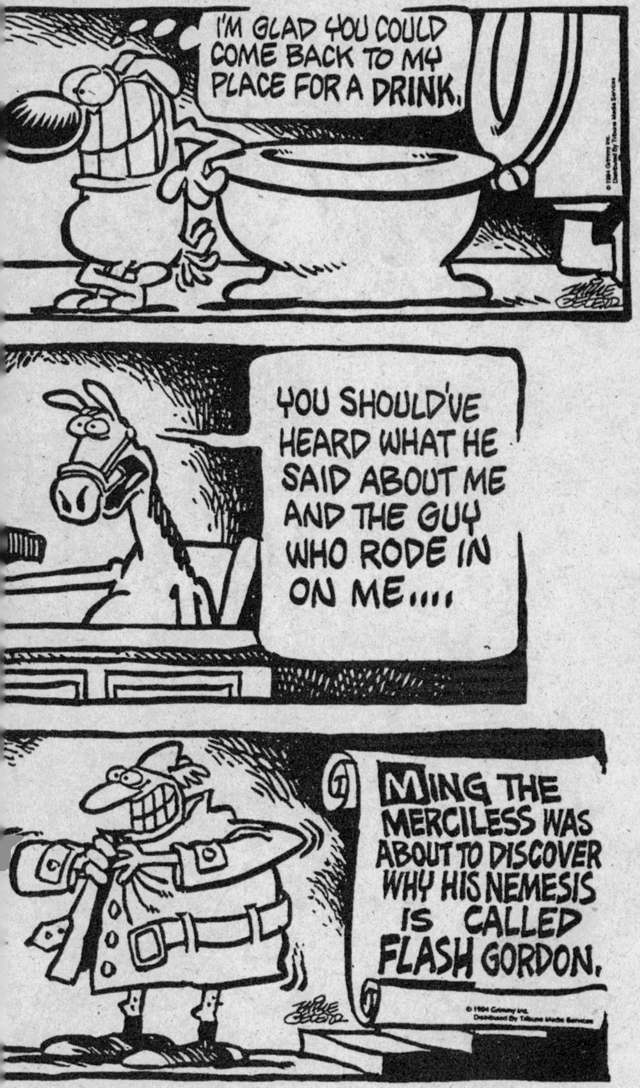
I'M GLAD YOU COULD COME BACK TO MY PLACE FOR A DRINK.
© 1994 Grimmy Inc. Distributed By Tribune Media Services
YOU SHOULD'VE HEARD WHAT HE SAID ABOUT ME AND THE GUY WHO RODE IN ON ME....
MING THE MERCILESS WAS ABOUT TO DISCOVER WHY HIS NEMESIS IS CALLED FLASH GORDON.
© 1994 Grimmy Inc. Distributed By Tribune Media Services

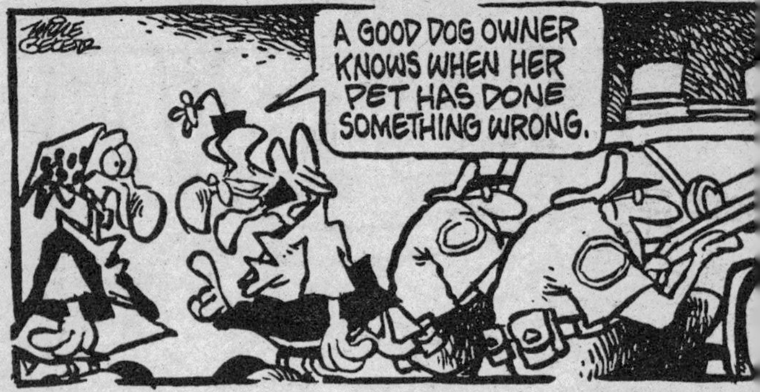
A GOOD DOG OWNER KNOWS WHEN HER PET HAS DONE SOMETHING WRONG.

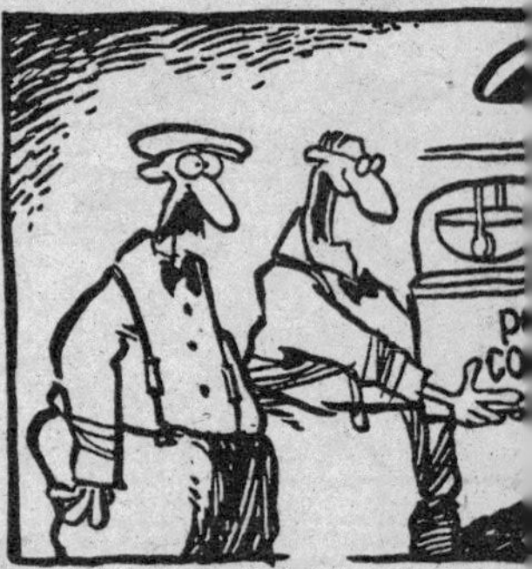

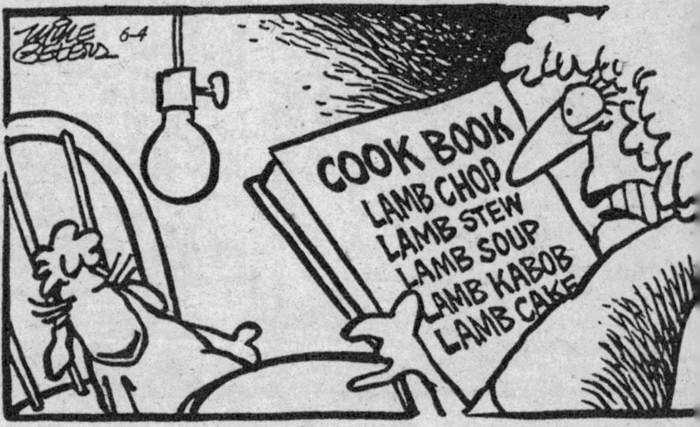
6-4
COOK BOOK
LAMB CHOP
LAMB STEW
LAMB SOUP
LAMB KABOB
LAMB CAKE

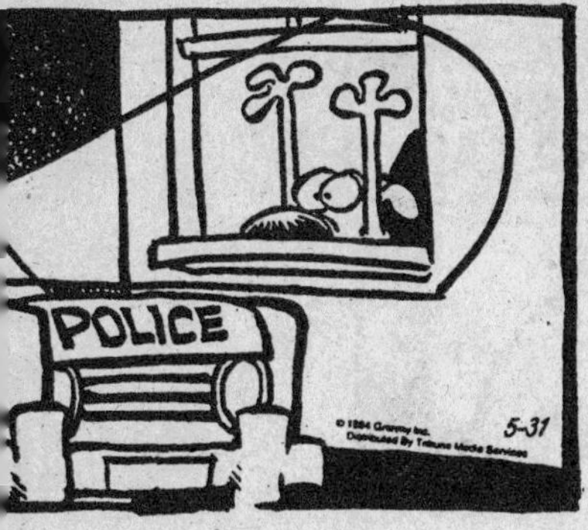
POLICE
5-31

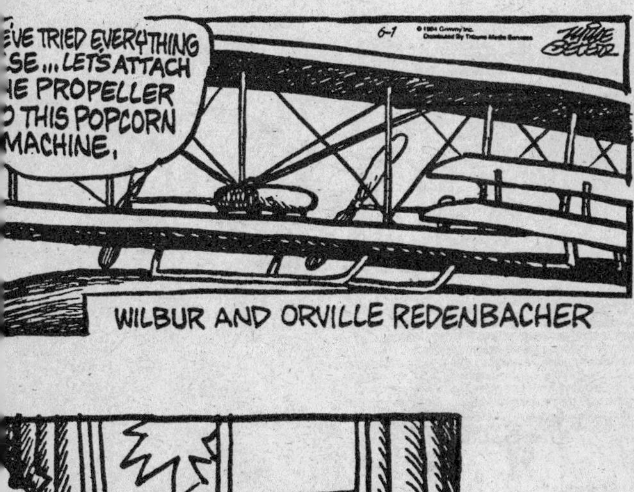
'VE TRIED EVERYTHING
SE... LET'S ATTACH
HE PROPELLER
O THIS POPCORN
MACHINE.
6-1

WILBUR AND ORVILLE REDENBACHER

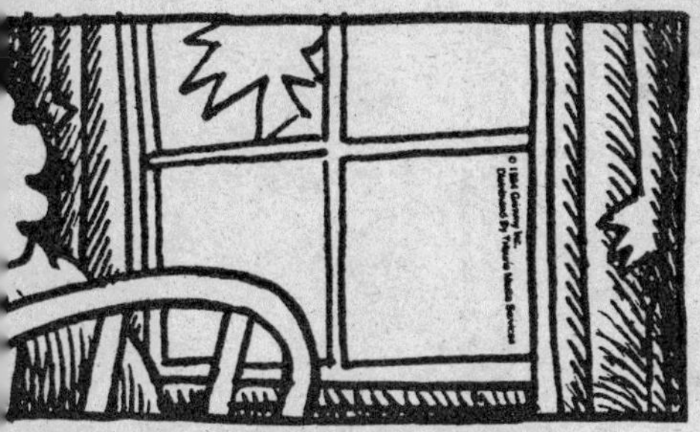

SHARI LEWIS DURING
THE LEAN YEARS

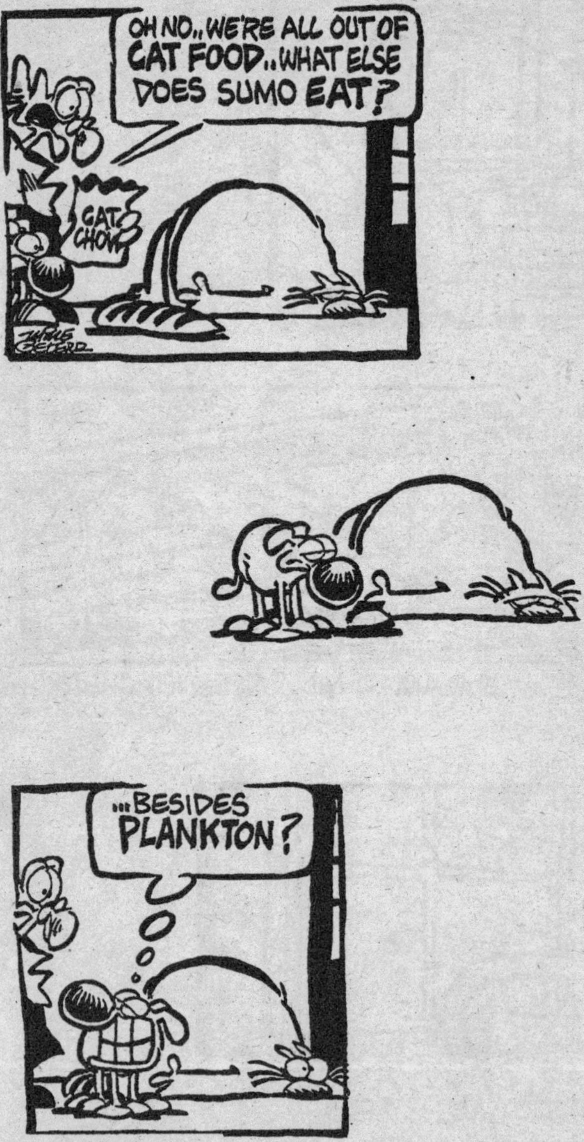
OH NO.. WE'RE ALL OUT OF CAT FOOD.. WHAT ELSE DOES SUMO EAT?
CAT CHOW
...BESIDES PLANKTON?

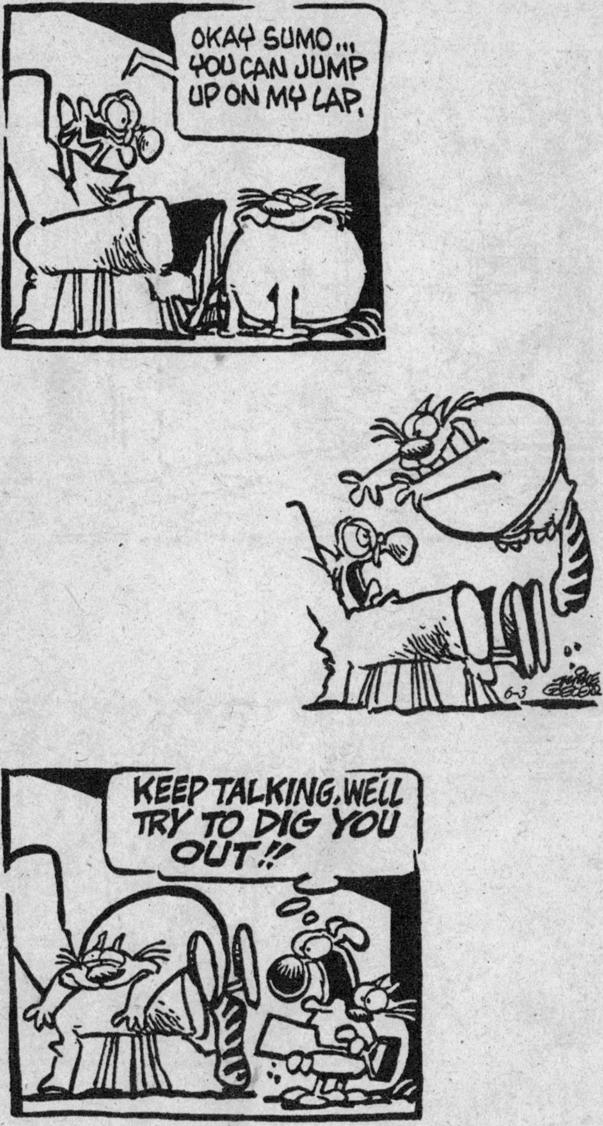
OKAY SUMO... YOU CAN JUMP UP ON MY LAP.
KEEP TALKING. WE'LL TRY TO DIG YOU OUT!!

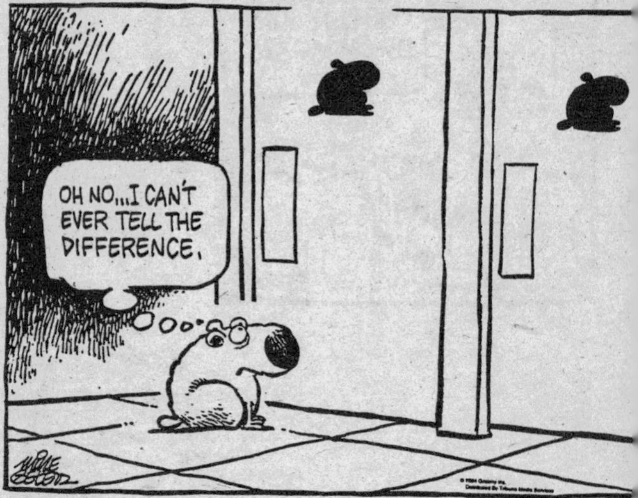
OH NO...I CAN'T EVER TELL THE DIFFERENCE.

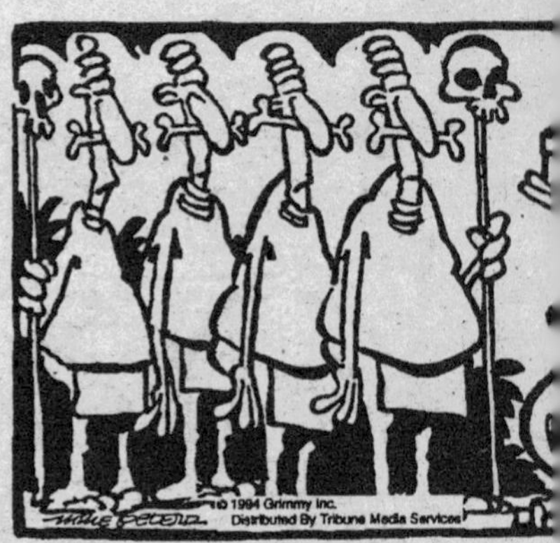
© 1994 Grimmy Inc.
Distributed By Tribune Media Services

GERBIL RESTROOMS

THERE MUST BE SOME MISTAKE, I SELL WEIGHT-LOSS PRODUCTS, PERHAPS YOU'VE HEARD OF ME....

THAT NIGHT, THE WHOLE TRIBE WENT ON THE JENNY CRAIG DIET....

10/1

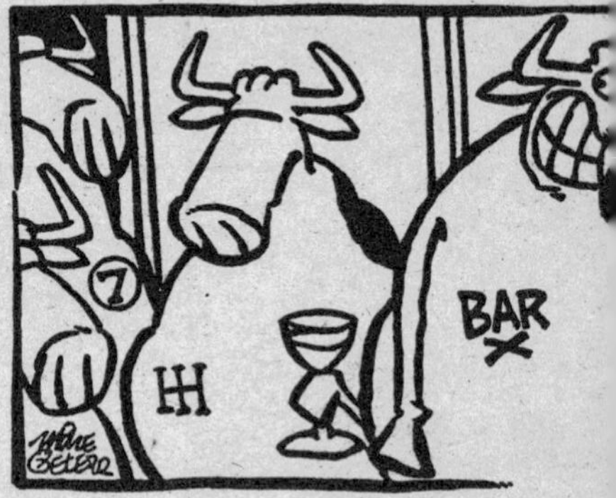
7
BAR

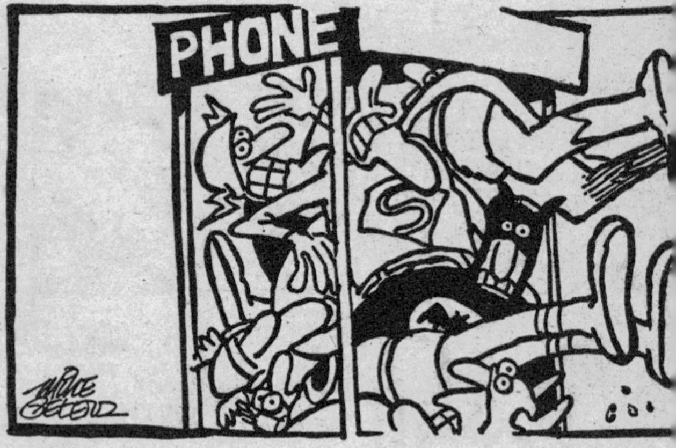
PHONE

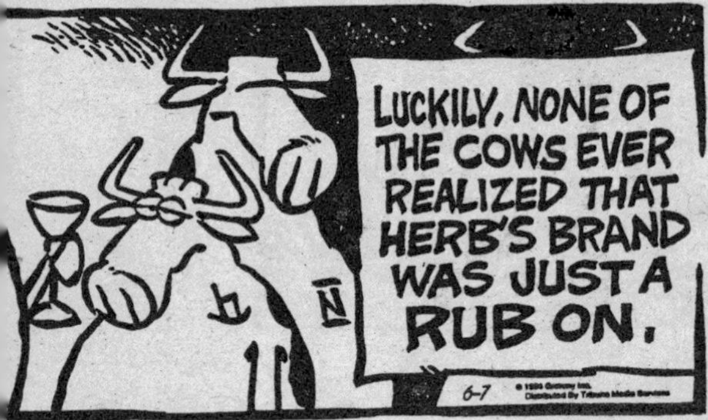
LUCKILY, NONE OF THE COWS EVER REALIZED THAT HERB'S BRAND WAS JUST A RUB ON.
6-7

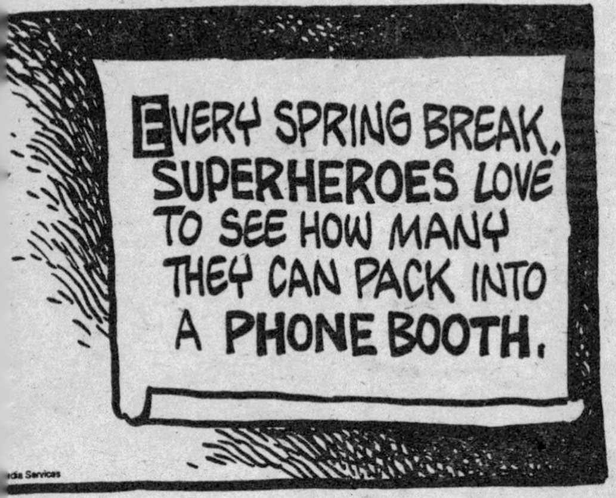
EVERY SPRING BREAK, SUPERHEROES LOVE TO SEE HOW MANY THEY CAN PACK INTO A PHONE BOOTH.
dia Services

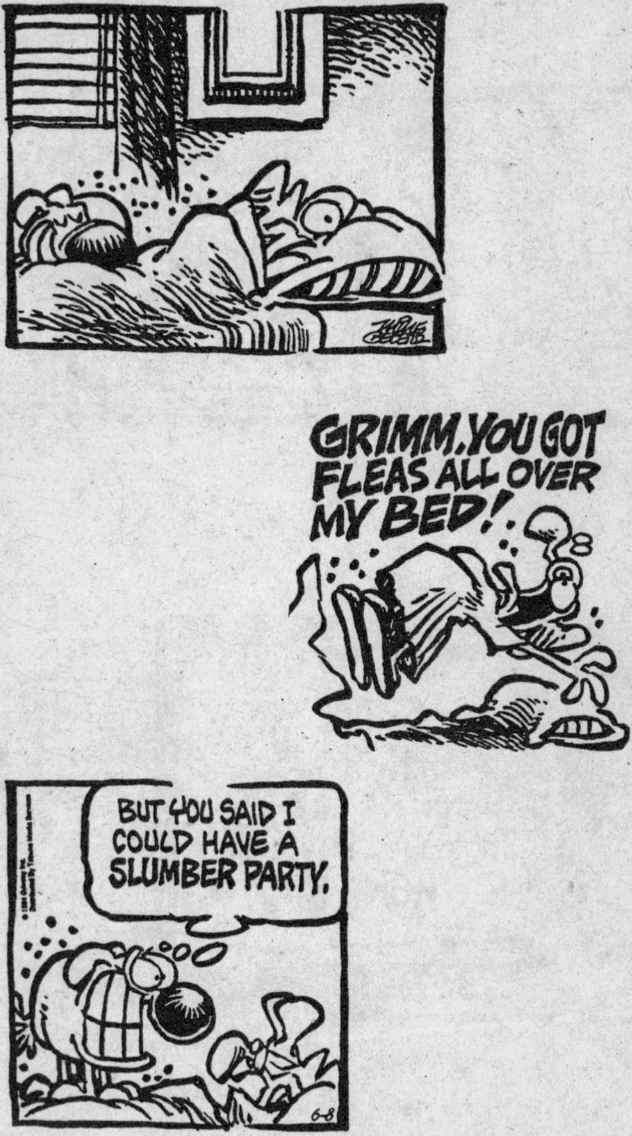
GRIMM, YOU GOT FLEAS ALL OVER MY BED!
BUT YOU SAID I COULD HAVE A SLUMBER PARTY.

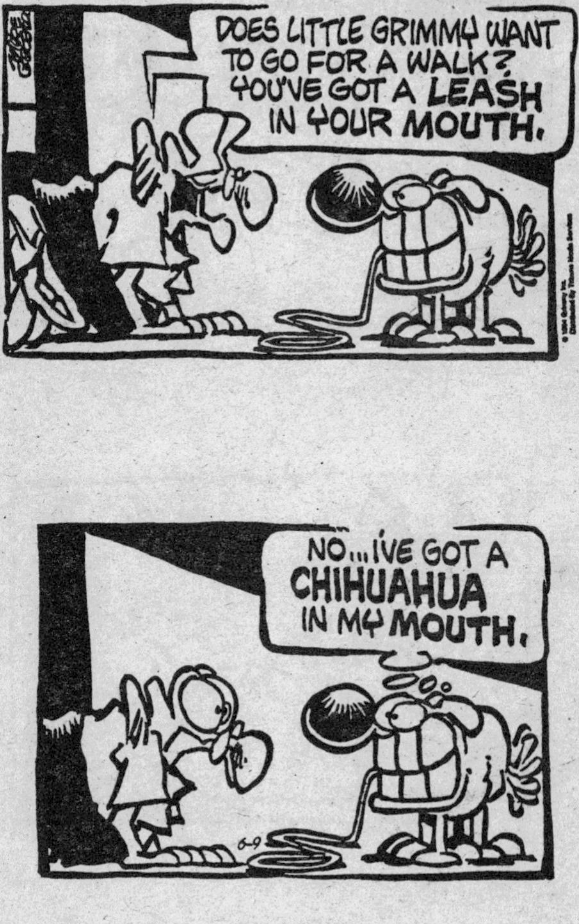
DOES LITTLE GRIMMY WANT TO GO FOR A WALK? YOU'VE GOT A LEASH IN YOUR MOUTH.
NO... I'VE GOT A CHIHUAHUA IN MY MOUTH.

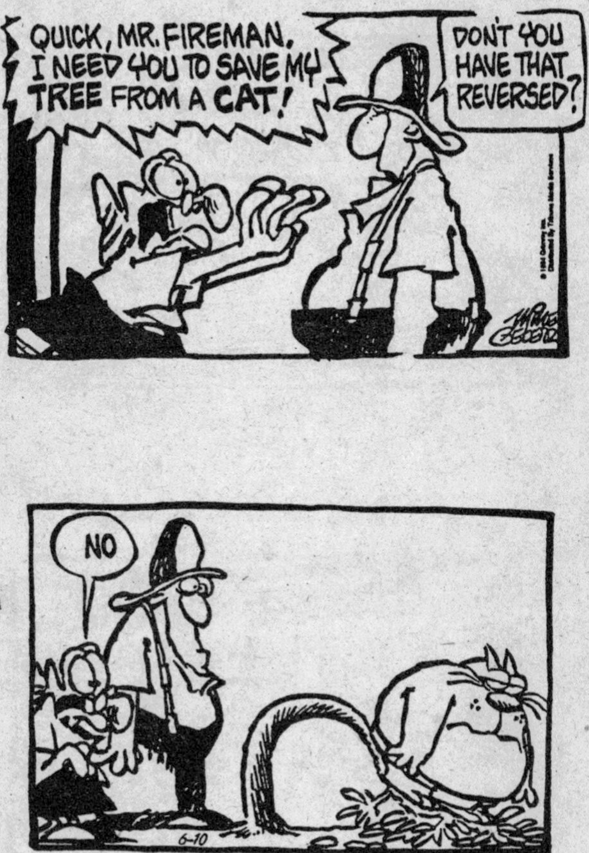
QUICK, MR. FIREMAN. I NEED YOU TO SAVE MY TREE FROM A CAT!
DON'T YOU HAVE THAT REVERSED?
NO
6-10

I LOVE SPRINGS.
YOU MEAN YOU LOVE SPRING.
BOING
NO, I MEAN I LOVE SPRINGS.
6-11

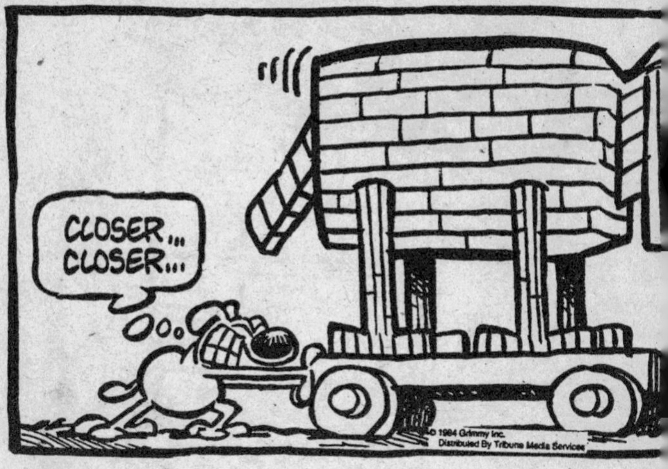
CLOSER...
CLOSER...
© 1984 Grimmy Inc.
Distributed By Tribune Media Services

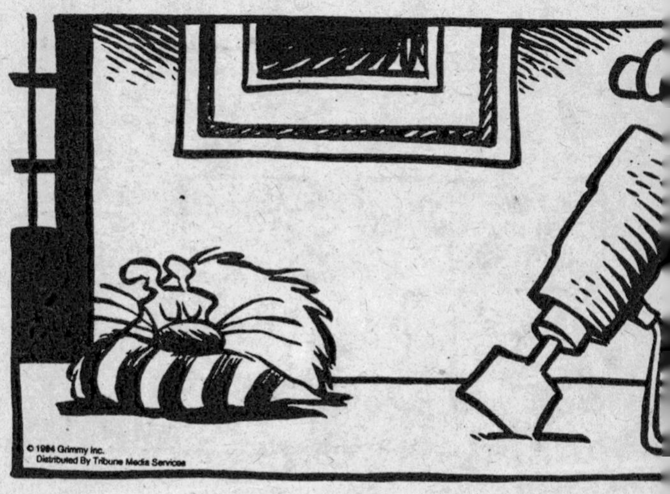
© 1984 Grimmy Inc.
Distributed By Tribune Media Services

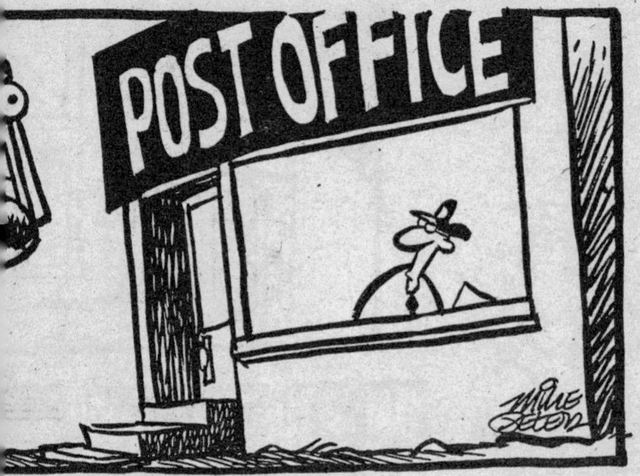
POST OFFICE

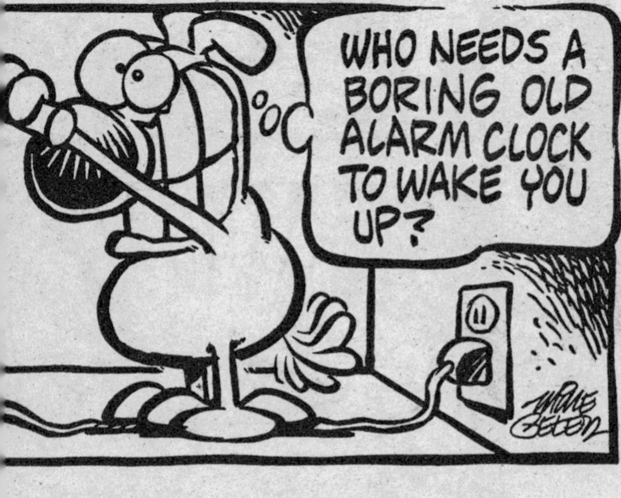
WHO NEEDS A BORING OLD ALARM CLOCK TO WAKE YOU UP?

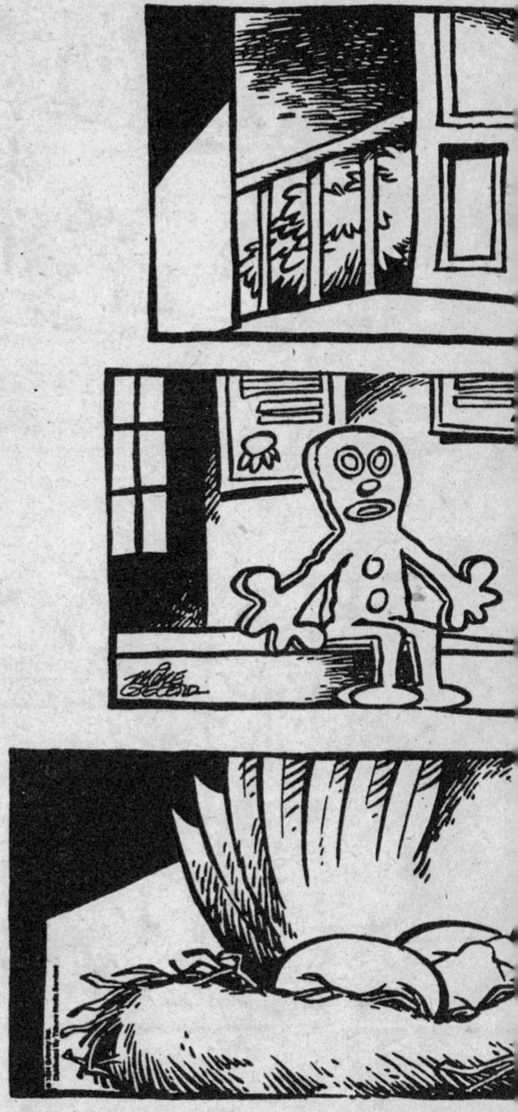

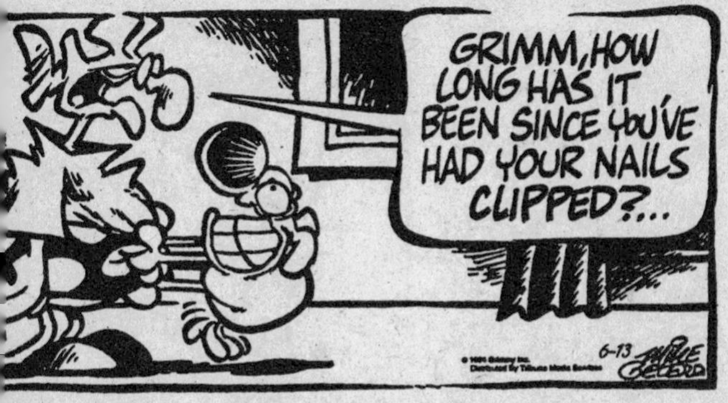
GRIMM, HOW LONG HAS IT BEEN SINCE YOU'VE HAD YOUR NAILS CLIPPED?...
6-13

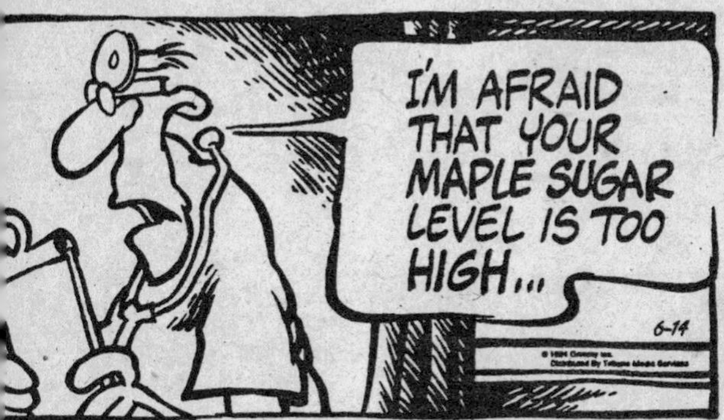
I'M AFRAID THAT YOUR MAPLE SUGAR LEVEL IS TOO HIGH...
6-14

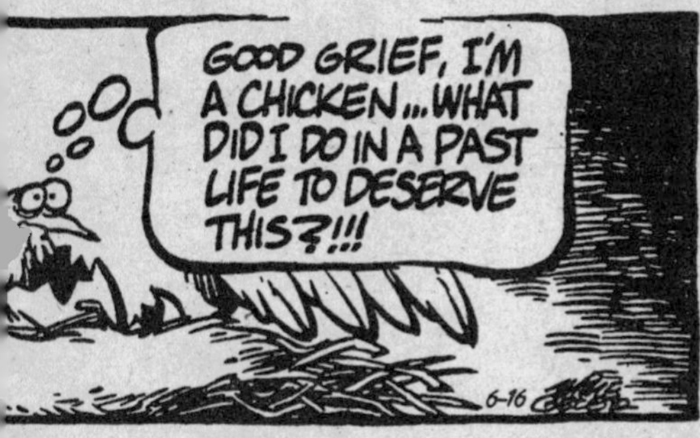
GOOD GRIEF, I'M A CHICKEN... WHAT DID I DO IN A PAST LIFE TO DESERVE THIS?!!!
6-16

EINCARNATION OF COL. SANDERS

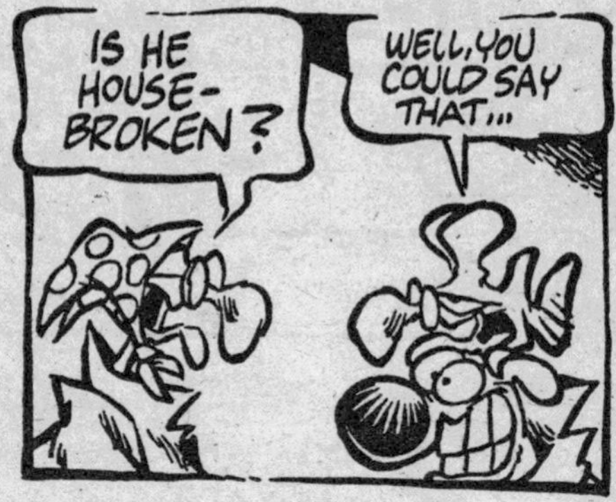
IS HE HOUSE-BROKEN?
WELL, YOU COULD SAY THAT...

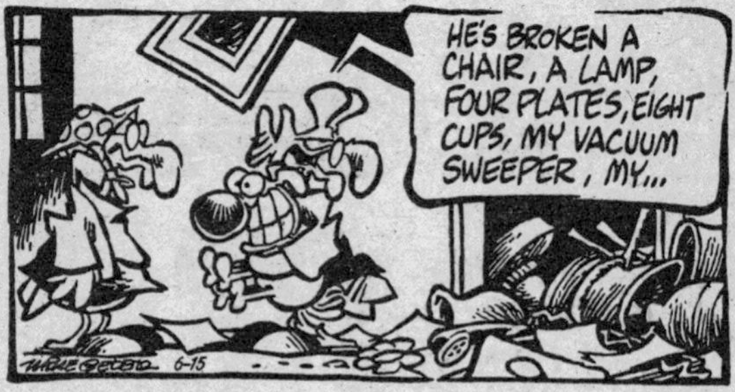
HE'S BROKEN A CHAIR, A LAMP, FOUR PLATES, EIGHT CUPS, MY VACUUM SWEEPER, MY...

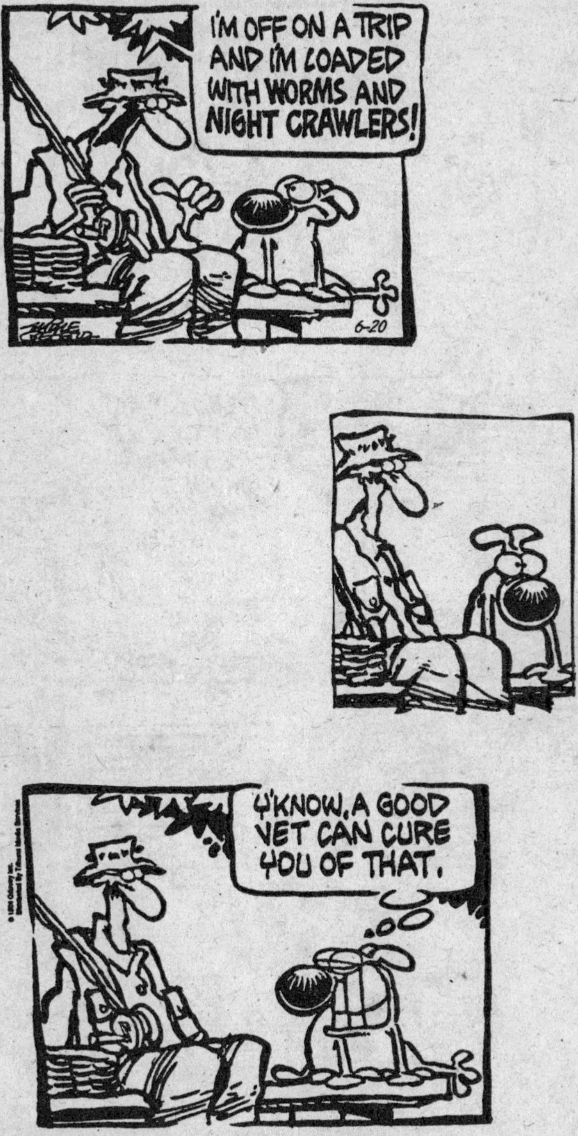
I'M OFF ON A TRIP AND I'M LOADED WITH WORMS AND NIGHT CRAWLERS!
6-20
Y'KNOW, A GOOD VET CAN CURE YOU OF THAT.

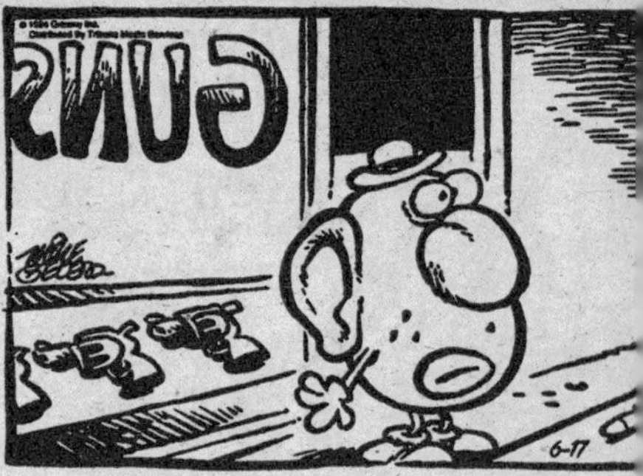
GUNS
6-17

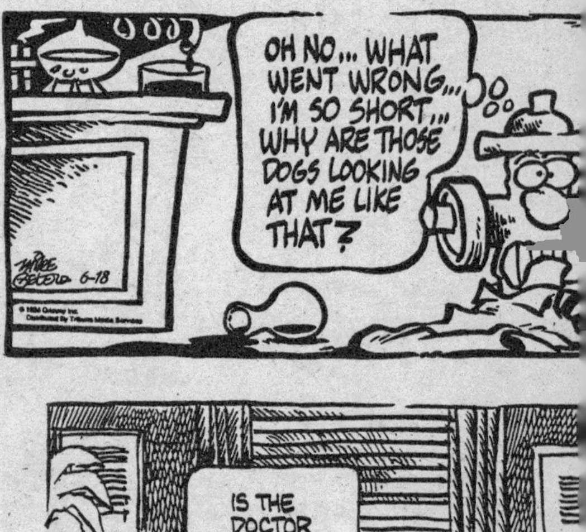
OH NO... WHAT WENT WRONG... I'M SO SHORT... WHY ARE THOSE DOGS LOOKING AT ME LIKE THAT?
6-18

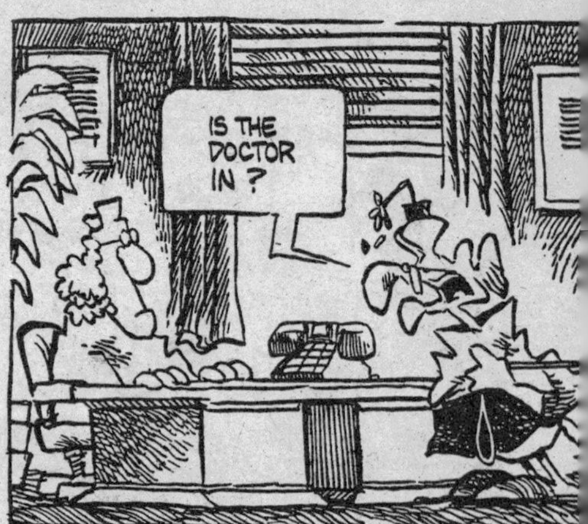
IS THE DOCTOR IN ?

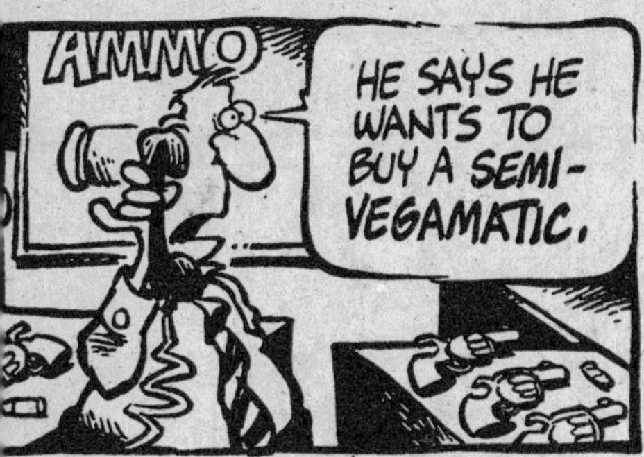
AMMO
HE SAYS HE WANTS TO BUY A SEMI-VEGAMATIC.

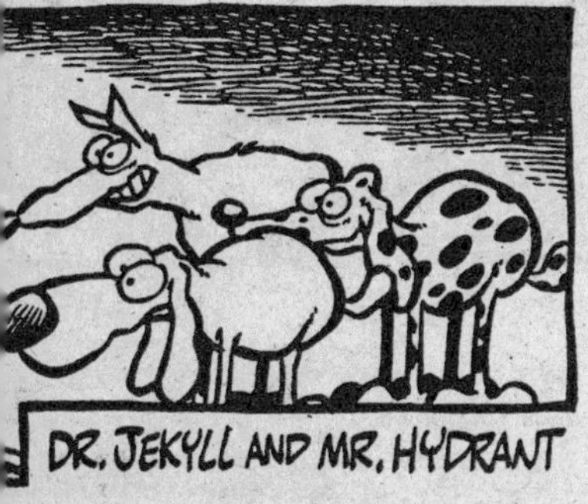

DR. JEKYLL AND MR. HYDRANT

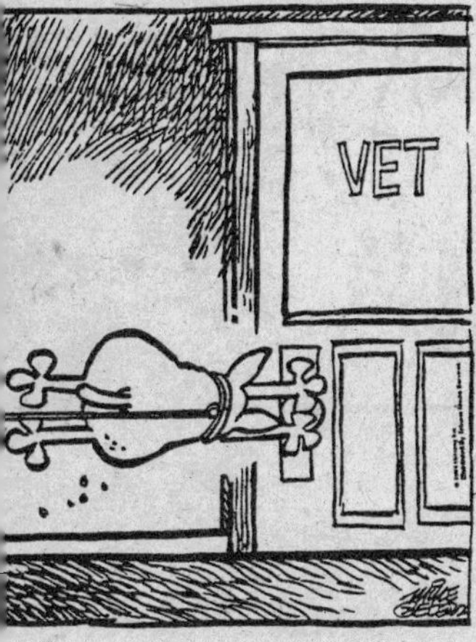
VET

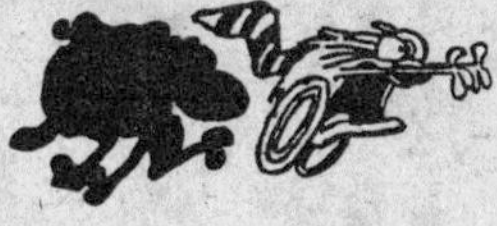

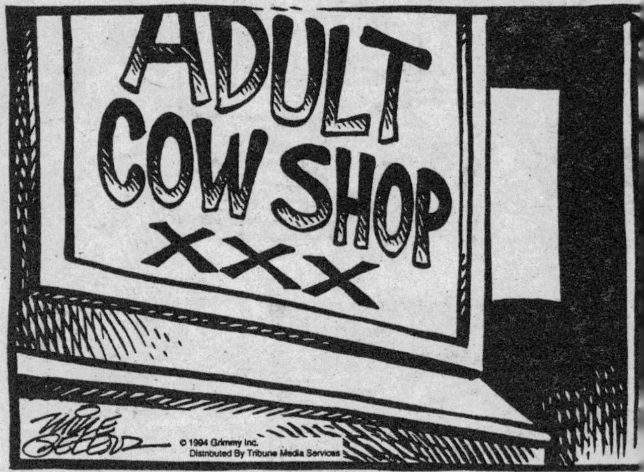
ADULT COW SHOP
XXX
© 1994 Grimmy Inc.
Distributed By Tribune Media Services

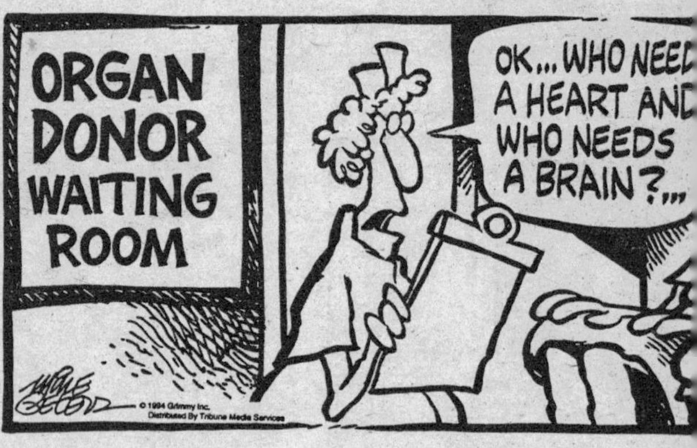
ORGAN DONOR WAITING ROOM
OK... WHO NEED
A HEART AND
WHO NEEDS
A BRAIN?...
© 1994 Grimmy Inc.
Distributed By Tribune Media Services

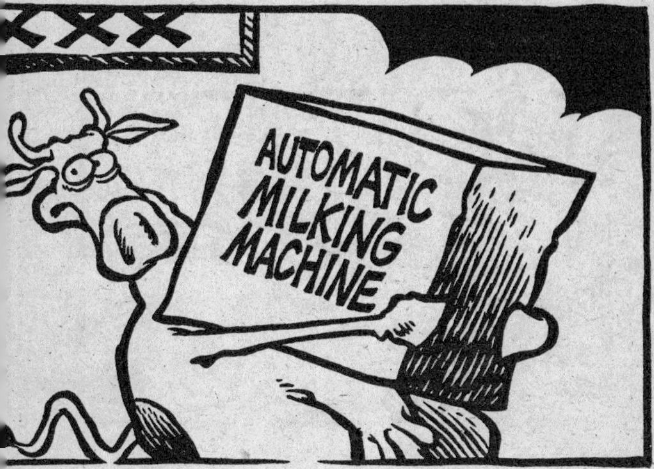
AUTOMATIC
MILKING
MACHINE

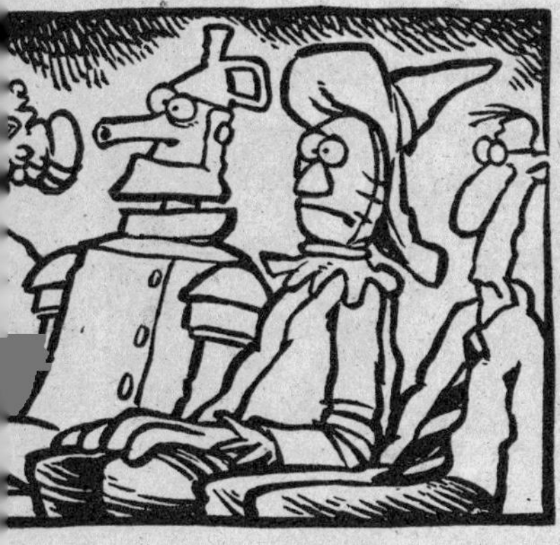

I GOT IT. I GOT IT.
6-21
I HATE THESE NEW LONG-DISTANCE FRISBEES.

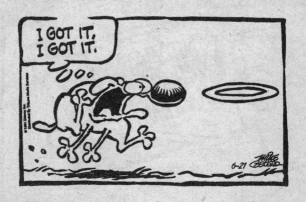

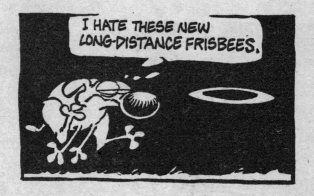

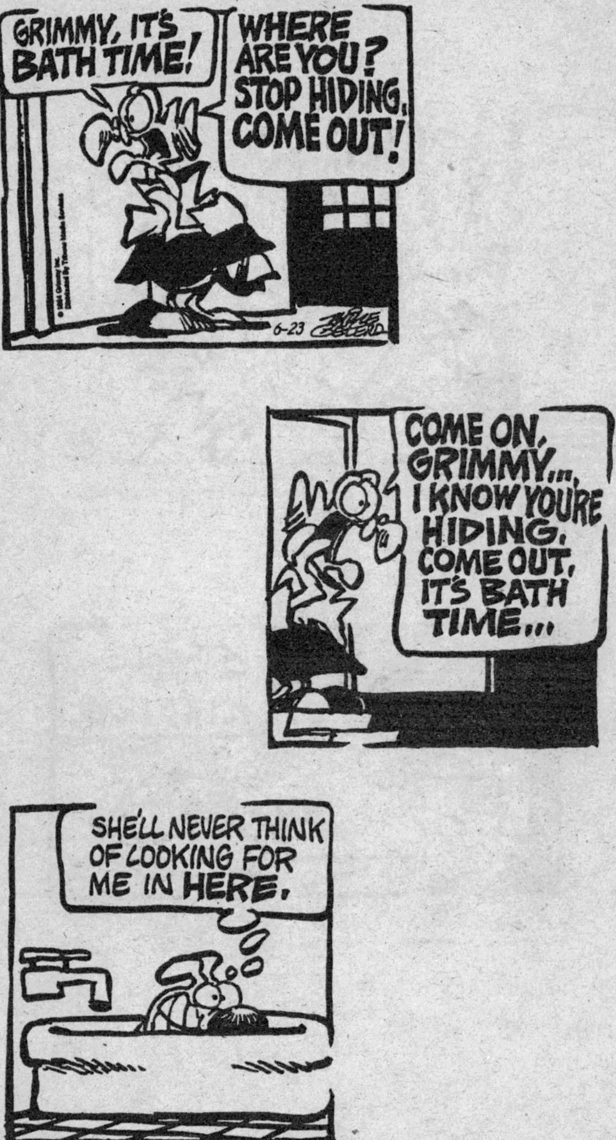
GRIMMY, IT'S BATH TIME!
WHERE ARE YOU? STOP HIDING, COME OUT!
6-23
COME ON, GRIMMY..., I KNOW YOU'RE HIDING, COME OUT, IT'S BATH TIME...
SHE'LL NEVER THINK OF LOOKING FOR ME IN HERE.

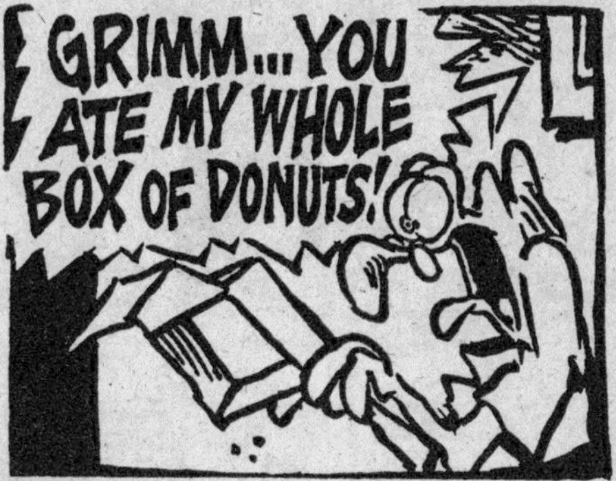
GRIMM...YOU ATE MY WHOLE BOX OF DONUTS!

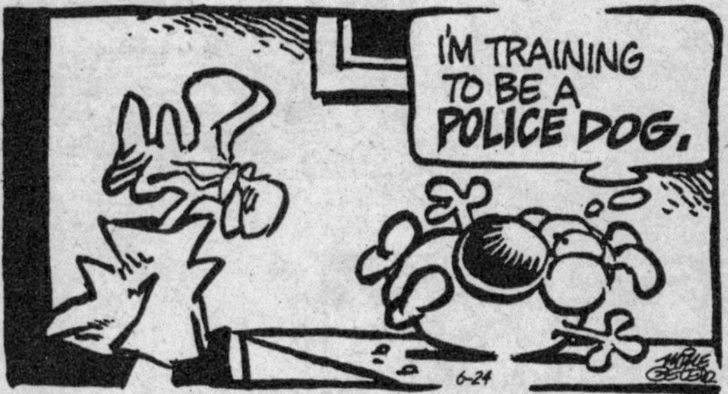
I'M TRAINING TO BE A POLICE DOG.
6-24

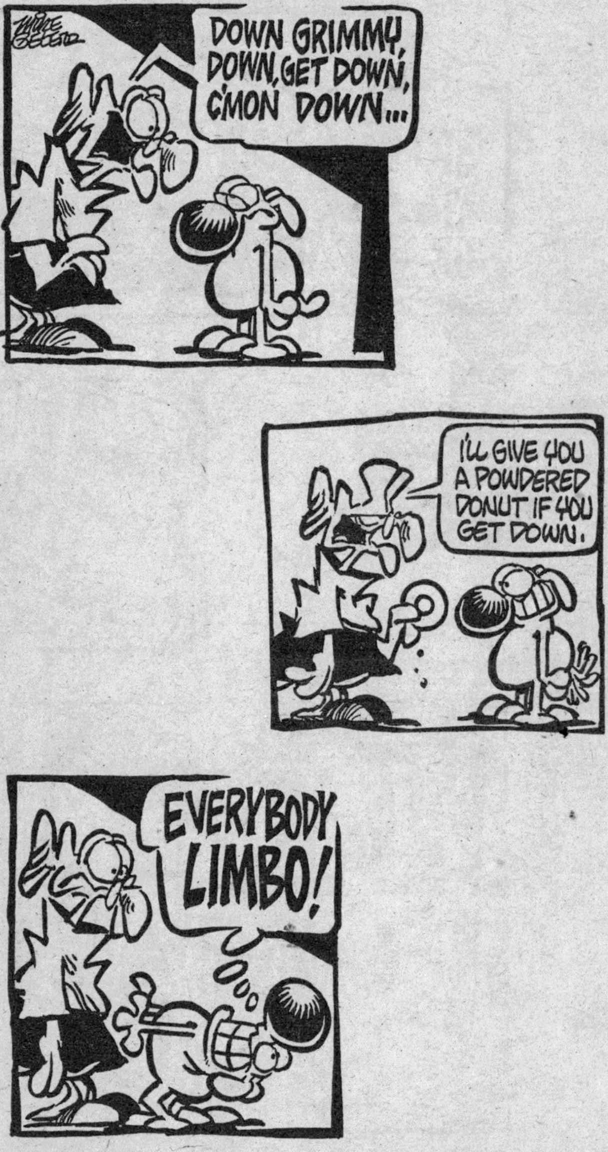
DOWN GRIMMY, DOWN, GET DOWN, C'MON DOWN...
I'LL GIVE YOU A POWDERED DONUT IF YOU GET DOWN.
EVERYBODY LIMBO!
OOO

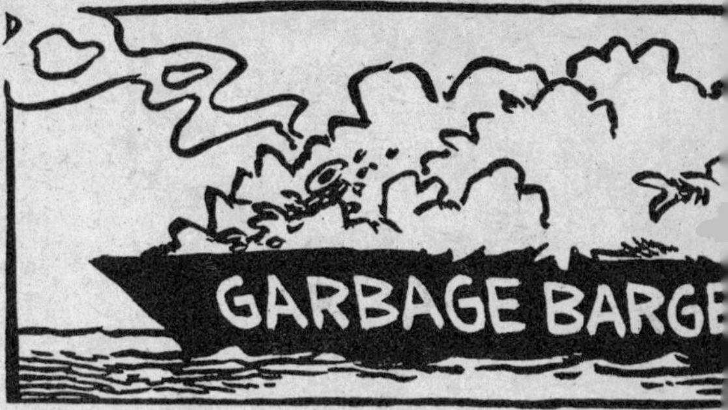
GARBAGE BARGE

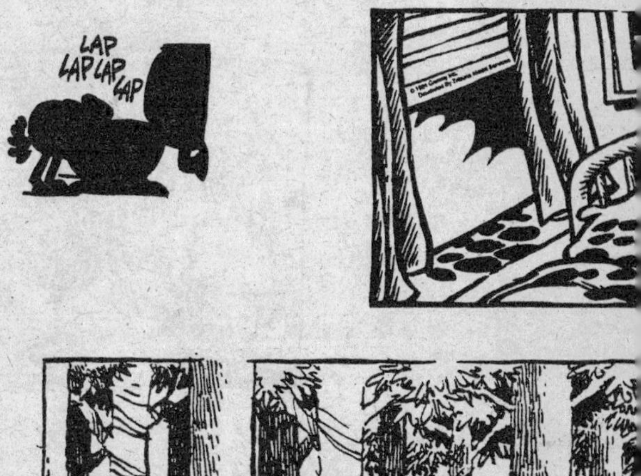
LAP
LAP LAP LAP

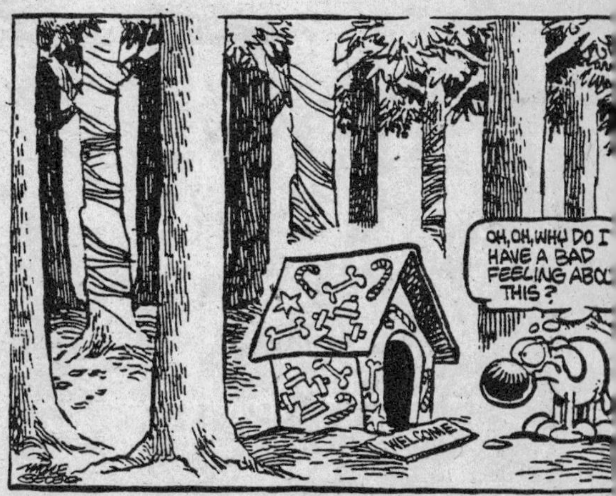
OH, OH, WHY DO I
HAVE A BAD
FEELING ABO
THIS?
WELCOME

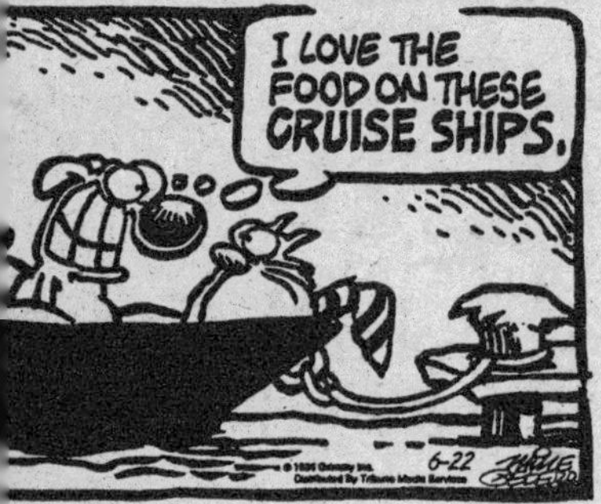
I LOVE THE FOOD ON THESE CRUISE SHIPS.
6-22

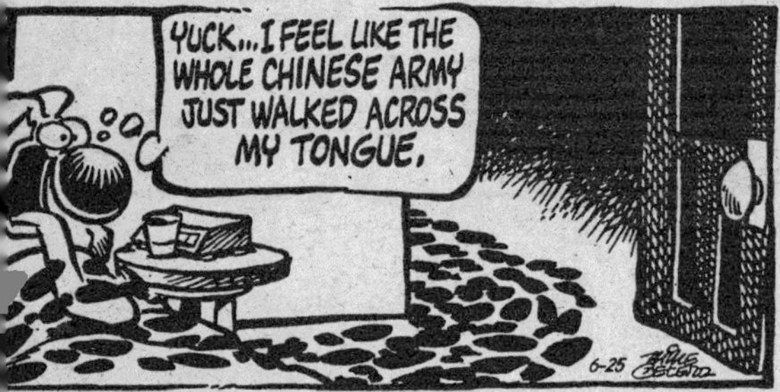
YUCK...I FEEL LIKE THE WHOLE CHINESE ARMY JUST WALKED ACROSS MY TONGUE.
6-25

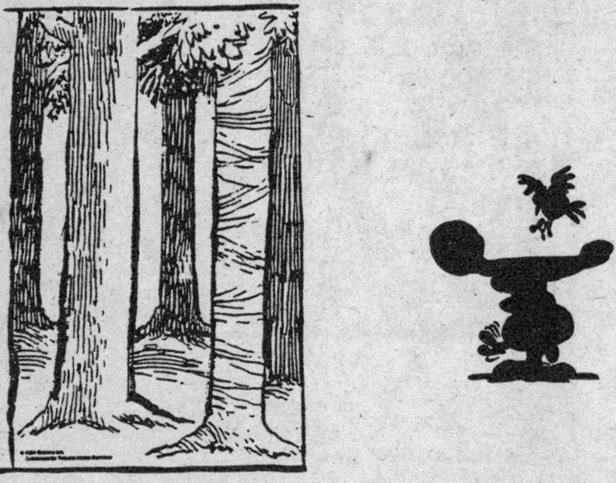

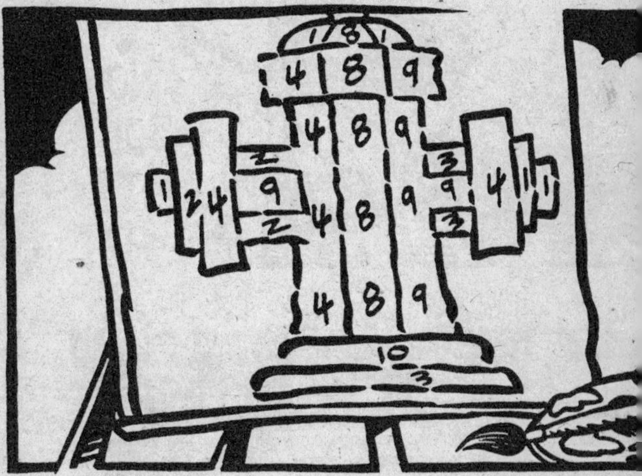

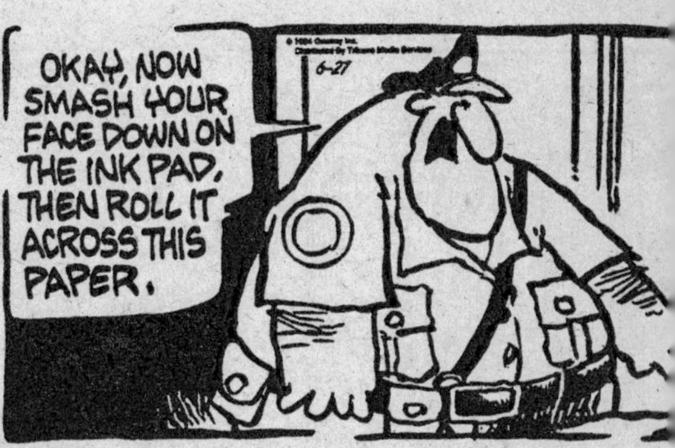
OKAY, NOW SMASH YOUR FACE DOWN ON THE INK PAD, THEN ROLL IT ACROSS THIS PAPER.
6-27

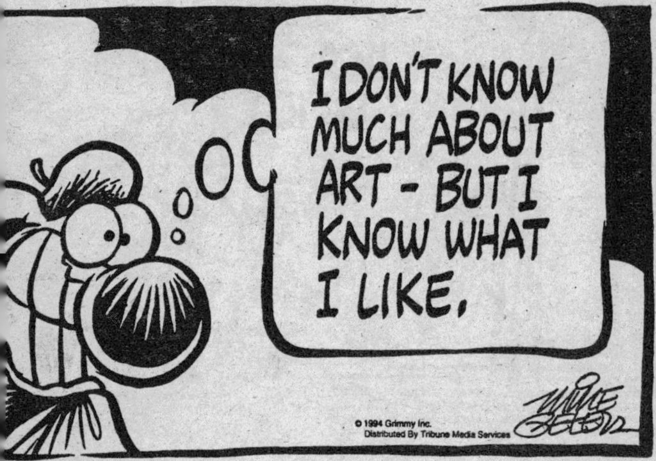
I DON'T KNOW MUCH ABOUT ART - BUT I KNOW WHAT I LIKE.
© 1994 Grimmy Inc.
Distributed By Tribune Media Services

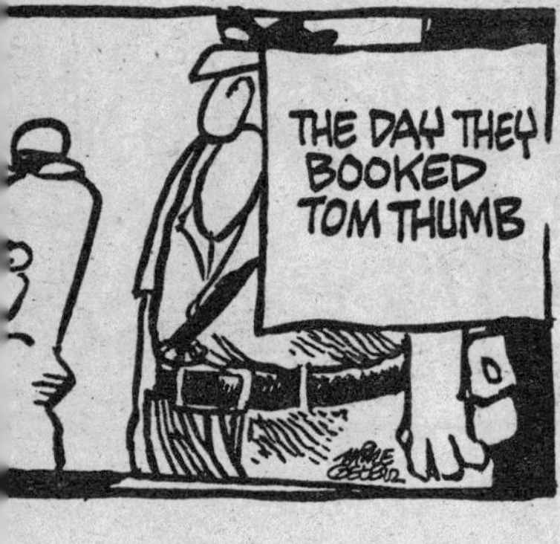
THE DAY THEY BOOKED TOM THUMB

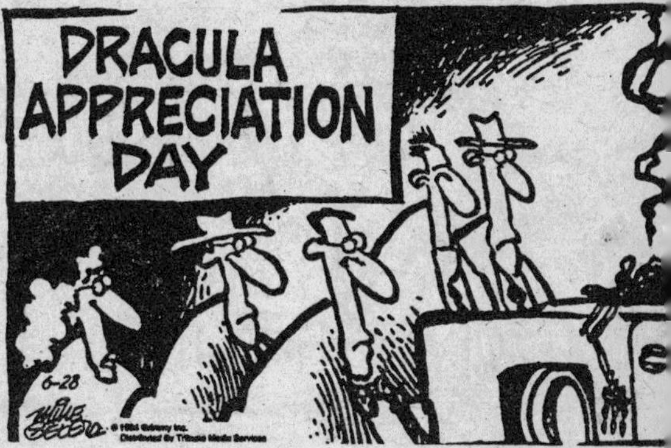
DRACULA APPRECIATION DAY
6-28

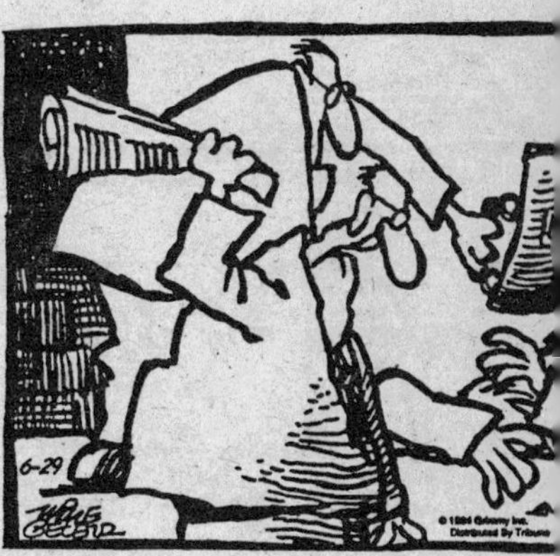
6-29

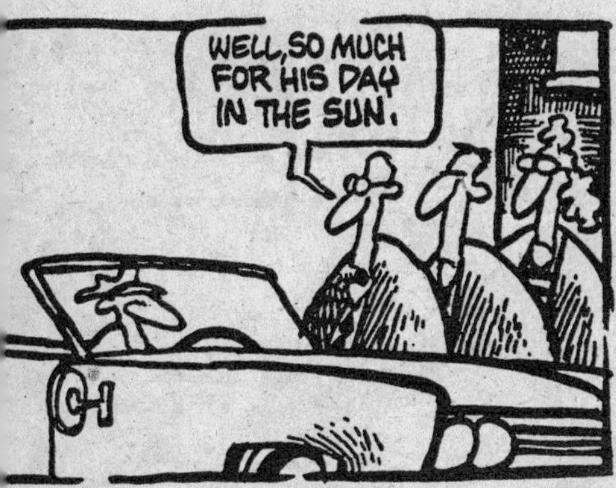
WELL, SO MUCH FOR HIS DAY IN THE SUN.

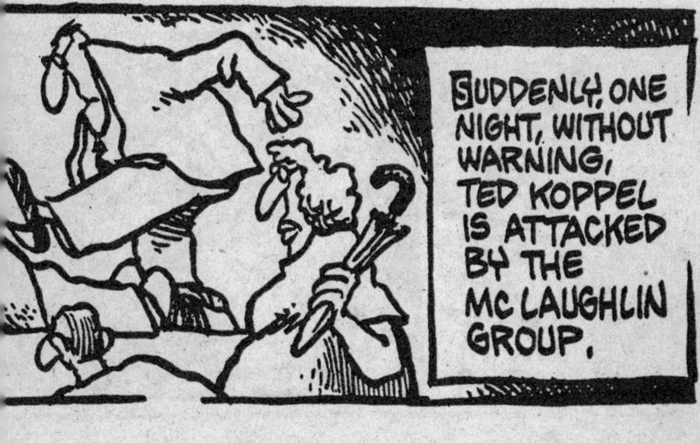
SUDDENLY, ONE NIGHT, WITHOUT WARNING, TED KOPPEL IS ATTACKED BY THE McLAUGHLIN GROUP.

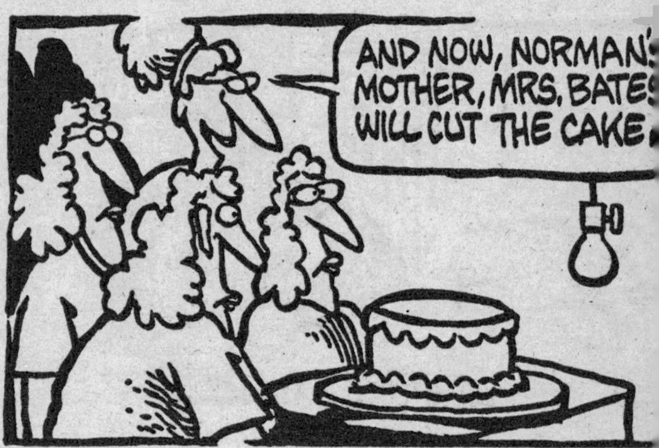
AND NOW, NORMAN'S MOTHER, MRS. BATES WILL CUT THE CAKE

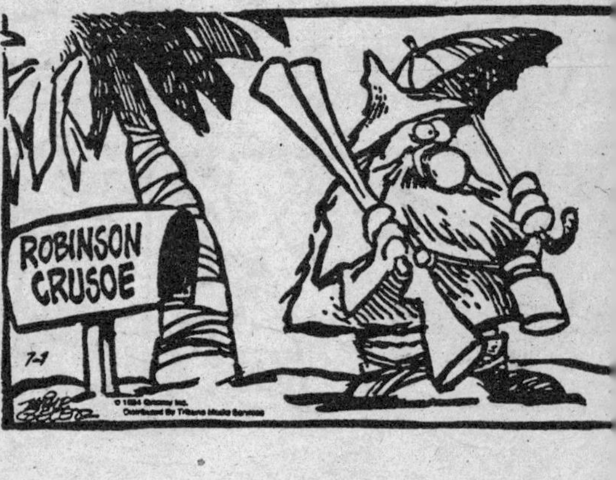
ROBINSON CRUSOE
7-1

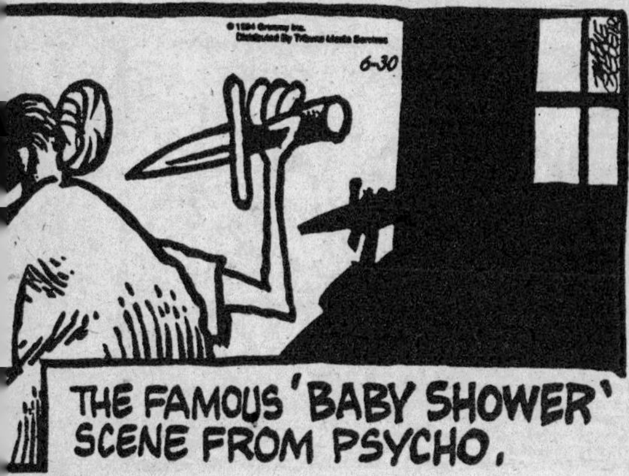
6-30

THE FAMOUS 'BABY SHOWER' SCENE FROM PSYCHO.

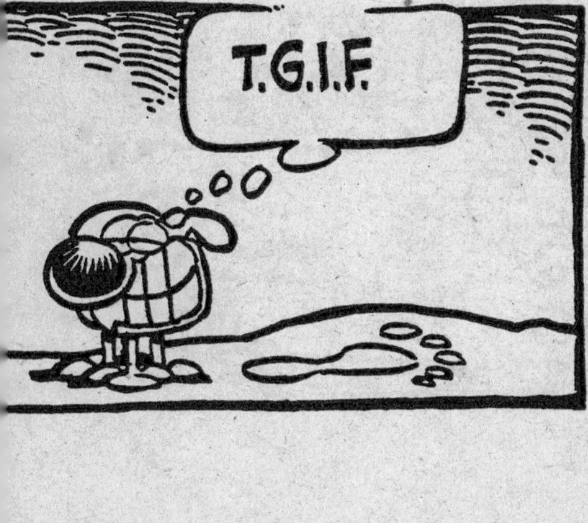
T.G.I.F.

GRIMMY!
...YOU'RE SUPPOSED TO PEEL THE BANANA BEFORE YOU EAT IT.
7-2

WHERE ARE THE GOODS?

MANY OF OUR READERS ASK HOW THEY CAN BUY GRIMMY MERCHANDISE.

HERE IS A LIST OF LICENSEES IN THE UNITED STATES AND CANADA THAT CARRY GREAT STUFF!

GIVE THEM A CALL FOR YOUR LOCAL DISTRIBUTOR.

WWW.GRIMMY.COM

The Antioch Company 888 Dayton St. Yellow Springs, OH 45387	PH 800/543-2397 Bookmarks, Wallet Cards, **"Largely Literary"** products: T-Shirts, Mugs, Journals, Pens, Notepads, Bookplates, Bookmarks
Avalanche Publishing 1093 Bedmar St. Carson, CA 90746	PH 310/223-1600 365 Day Box Calendar-Year 2000 www.avalanchepub.com
Classcom, Inc. 770 Bertrand Montreal, Quebec Canada H4M1V9	PH 514/747-9492 Desk Art
C.T.I. 22160 North Pepper Rd. Barrington, IL 60010	PH 800/284-5605 Balloons, Coffee Mugs
F.X. Schmid/USA 1 Puzzle Lane Newton, NH 03858	PH 800/886-1236 Puzzles www.fxschmid.com
Gibson Greetings 2100 Section Rd. Cincinnati, OH 45237	PH 800/345-6521 Greeting Cards, Party Papers, Gift Wrap etc... www.greetst.com
Linda Jones Enterprises 17771 Mitchell Irvine, CA 92614	PH 949/660-7791 Cels
MR. TEES 3225 Hartsfield Rd. Tallahassee, FL 32303	PH 850/574-3737 T-Shirts
Pomegranate 210 Classic Ct. Rohnert Park, CA 94928	PH 800/227-1428 Wall Year 2000 Calendars, Postcard Booklets www.pomegranate.com
Second Nature Software 1325 Officers' Row Vancouver, WA 98661	PH 360/737-4170 Screen Saver Program www.secondnature.com
TOR Books 175 Fifth Ave. New York, NY 10010	PH 212/388-0100 Paperback Books www.tor.com
Western Graphics 3535 W. 1st Avenue Eugene, OR 97402	PH 800/532-3303 Posters